Gilles Deleuze

An Introduction

This book offers a readable and compelling introduction to the work of one of the twentieth century's most important and elusive thinkers. Other books have tried to explain Deleuze in general terms. Todd May organizes his book around a central question at the heart of Deleuze's philosophy: how might one live? The author then goes on to explain how Deleuze offers a view of the cosmos as a living thing that provides ways of conducting our lives that we may not have dreamed of. Through this approach the full range of Deleuze's philosophy is covered.

Offering a lucid account of a highly technical philosophy, Todd May's introduction will be widely read among those in philosophy, political science, cultural studies, and French studies.

Todd May is Professor of Philosophy in the Department of Philosophy and Religion at Clemson University in South Carolina.

Gilles Deleuze

An Introduction

TODD MAY

Clemson University

CAMBRIDGE
UNIVERSITY PRESS

CAMBRIDGE UNIVERSITY PRESS
Cambridge, New York, Melbourne, Madrid, Cape Town,
Singapore, São Paulo, Delhi, Tokyo, Mexico City

Cambridge University Press
The Edinburgh Building, Cambridge CB2 8RU, UK

Published in the United States of America by Cambridge University Press, New York

www.cambridge.org
Information on this title: www.cambridge.org/9780521603843

First published 2005
Reprinted 2006 (twice), 2008

A catalogue record for this publication is available from the British Library

Library of Congress Cataloguing in Publication Data

May, Todd, 1955–
Gilles Deleuze : an introduction / Todd May.
p. cm.
Includes bibliographical references and index.
ISBN 0-521-84309-X — ISBN 0-521-60384-6 (pb.)
1. Deleuze, Gilles. 2. Philosophy, French – 20th century. I. Title.
B2430.D454M39   2004
194–dc22   2004045891

ISBN 978-0-521-84309-6 Hardback
ISBN 978-0-521-60384-3 Paperback

For Constantin Boundas
in gratitude for his patience and generosity

Contents

Acknowledgments

I would like to thank Gary Gutting, who paved the way for this book. Terence Moore, Stephanie Achard, and Sally Nicholls, at Cambridge University Press, have been a pleasure to work with. Three anonymous reviewers for the Press made important suggestions; I hope I have not betrayed their efforts in my revisions. Some of the pages on science in the third chapter are revisions of an article, "Deleuze, Difference, and Science," which appeared in a volume edited by Gary Gutting, *Continental Philosophy and Science*, published by Basil Blackwell in 2004. I appreciate their permission to modify and reprint those pages.

Gilles Deleuze

An Introduction

1

How Might One Live?

I

How might one live?

It's an odd question, in some sense; a question we don't ask ourselves very often. We get up in the morning, we brush our teeth, we crawl into our clothing, and burn our days as though it were impossible to live any other way, as though this particular life were the only one to be lived. As though the universe were so constructed that it required our lives to unfold in this way and in no other.

Of course that isn't what we tell ourselves. Our stories are always filled with choices, with crossroads and tangents and directions of our own making. Our lives' narratives, when we tell them to ourselves or to others, are steeped in the discarding of certain futures and the embrace of others, in the construction of a world that is to each of us uniquely our own because each of us has chosen it. But is that how we live? Is that how our lives, so often conforming, so often predictable, so often disappointing, come to be what they are?

How many of us ask ourselves, not once and for all time but frequently and at different times, *how might one live?* How many of us embrace that question, not only in our stories but in our actions, our projects, our commitments? How many of us open the door to the possibility that, however it is we are living, we might live otherwise?

II

Perhaps it is not up to each of us to ask this question. Perhaps, instead, it falls to philosophy, as a special study, to address it. What is the meaning of life? What are its purposes? How should one live? How might one live? These are questions that philosophers ask; they report their results to us, and we, if we choose, may read and assess them for their insights.

Philosophers rarely ask these questions. They rarely ask them in their work, and seem rarely to do so outside of it.

Part of the reason for this is historical. The twentieth century saw the division of Western philosophy into two distinct traditions. Britain and the United States embraced analytic philosophy, which treated these questions as though they fell outside the purview of philosophy. For some of those working in this tradition, the role of philosophy was to clarify the limits and range of scientific claims; for others, it was to understand the nature and functioning of language. The idea that philosophy might grapple with questions of our living was seen as a sort of conceptual confusion. Philosophy is to reflect on our knowledge and our language; it is to tell us how they work, or how they ought to work. To widen the tasks of philosophy to include a reflection on what we ought to become or might become is to introduce external, perhaps even incoherent, concerns into a discipline that seeks to achieve rigor and precision above all.

The historical situation for British and American philosophy has changed over the past thirty years. Since the publication of John Rawls' *A Theory of Justice*, it has become more nearly acceptable, in keeping with earlier periods in philosophy, to write and to think about the larger questions concerning our lives. The weight has lifted, but it has not been removed. Nearly a century of analytic work has instilled philosophical habits that are difficult to break. Those who are writing about normative matters still risk ridicule by those doing "hard" philosophy; they are still haunted by the fear of analytic failure. Too often, rather than harnessing the rigor of analytic philosophy to the task of asking these larger, more diffuse questions, instead the questions themselves are sacrificed or amputated in order to preserve the rigor of the method.

The other tradition in twentieth-century philosophy has come to be called the Continental tradition, since it focuses particularly on works written in France, Germany, and to a lesser extent Italy. In this tradition, the question of how one might live has never been lost, even though at times it has been eclipsed by other concerns. The major thinkers in this tradition, from Martin Heidegger through Jean-Paul Sartre and Maurice Merleau-Ponty to Michel Foucault and Jürgen Habermas, are never far from questions about the nature and possibilities of our living. And yet, here in the United States, where Continentally oriented philosophers are often studying the works of these thinkers, there is a tendency toward specialization that blunts the power of the larger questions. Perhaps because in so many other disciplines, the academy values the small nuance, the concrete accomplishment, the incremental result, many Continentally oriented philosophers are wont to spend less time engaged with the larger questions that animate a thinker's work. Instead they become engaged in the interpretation of some small corner of thought, an assessment of the accuracy of X's rendering of Y's interpretation of some marginal aspect of Z's work. (I am as guilty of this as are any of my philosophical colleagues, and so any fingers pointed here are directed also at me.)

In this book, I would like to hold out against that tendency and offer an interpretation of Gilles Deleuze that, even when weaving together details of his thought, remains mindful of and oriented toward the one question that is never far from his texts: how might one live? Although his thought is among the most esoteric, and even obscure, of recent thinkers, it is, rightly seen, nothing other than an engagement with that question. In a world that holds banality to be a virtue and originality a disease, Deleuze never stops asking the question of what other possibilities life holds open to us, or, more specifically, of how we might think about things in ways that would open up new regions for living. "*We do not even know of what a body is capable*, says Spinoza."[1]

III

The question of *how might one live* is not always the question that has been asked in philosophy by those who are concerned with how our lives might go. It is a question that has emerged over the course of the

---

[1] Deleuze, *Expressionism in Philosophy: Spinoza*, p. 226.

twentieth century, in the wake created by thinkers such as Friedrich Nietzsche and Sartre.

In ancient philosophy, the question was: *How should one live?* As the philosopher Bernard Williams has written, it is Socrates' question. "It is not a trivial question, Socrates said: what we are talking about is how one should live."[2] The question of how one should live involves a particular way of approaching life. It views life as having a shape: a life – a human life – is a whole that might be approached by way of asking how it should unfold. What is the course a human life should take? What are the best pursuits for a human being and how should those pursuits be arranged? What is the proper role for human beings in the universe?

Over the course of the modern period, the question *How should one live?* has been gradually replaced by another one. By the late eighteenth century, philosophers such as Immanuel Kant and Jeremy Bentham are addressing a different question. No longer is the concern with how one should live, with the shape one's life should take. Now the question is *How should one act?*

On the surface, it may seem that the question of how one should act is the same as that of how one should live. One lives through one's acts, does one not? And if so, then the shape of one's life will be nothing more than the sum of one's acts. These are not two different questions, they are instead two different forms of the same question.

Appearances here are deceiving. There are two significant differences behind the question asked by the ancients and that asked by the moderns that inflect the answers to these questions in different directions. First, for the ancients, the question of how one should live is asked within a context that assumes the existence of a cosmological order to which a good life must conform. A human life does not exist divorced from the cosmological whole within which it is embedded. It has a role to play that ought to converge with or at least complement the movement of the rest of the universe. For Plato, that role consists in seeking the Good; for Aristotle it is a matter of living out a specifically human teleology. Neither doubts, nor do others, such as the Stoics or the Epicureans, doubt, that the universe has an order to it, a stability and a general form that ought to be mirrored or conformed to by the lives of human beings.

[2] Williams, *Ethics and the Limits of Philosophy*, p. 1.

Modern philosophy writes within a context that jettisons the guiding assumption of a cosmological order. This does not mean that there is no God or that God has no efficacy in shaping the universe. The traces of God's work remain salient everywhere. It is the role of the human being that has changed. No longer does a human life find its significance in a larger order of which it is a part. Rather, a life is judged on its own merits. It answers to God or to the moral law, not to any order in which it might be embedded. Men and women stand alone before their acts and before the judge to whom those acts are submitted. There is no larger whole (or at least no whole larger than one's society) that requires one's participation.

This change has been known as the rise of individualism or alternatively the rise of the subject in modern philosophy.

The second change is inseparable from the first. We might call it the emergence of a democratic philosophy. Where there is order there is often hierarchy, and there is hierarchy in ancient order. Not only does each creature have a *place* in the cosmological order; it also has a *status*. That status involves dominance over creatures that lie below it and submission to those above. Slaves are to submit to their masters, women to their husbands. In this order, humans, particularly free males, have a privileged status in the cosmological order. Nevertheless, they too must submit to the larger whole of the cosmos itself and to those elements in the cosmos that lie above them. (One might take Plato's Good to be such an element.)

The modern period, in cutting adrift from the ancient moorings in a cosmological order, also frees itself from the hierarchies of dominance and submission inherent in that order. It casts aside the assumption of a cosmological higher and lower. Individualism is not simply a matter of divorcing oneself from the inherence in a cosmological role; it is also a divorce from the status conferred upon one inhabiting that role. With this divorce, we can glimpse the opening toward democracy and equal citizenship toward which we are still striving today.

By withdrawing allegiance to a cosmological order and by leveling out the status of human beings, the modern period becomes less concerned with the overall shape of one's life. It does not matter what the whole of a life looks like; it matters whether one is acting in the right way, whether one is fulfilling one's obligations. I no longer have to seek my rightful place in the order of things. Instead I must ask what my proper actions are, those that, as a member of society and as an individual before God, I am required to perform.

My actions, then, are distinct from my life as a whole. In fact, in the modern period the concern with one's life as a whole is diminished. Some philosophers have taken this languishing of concern with a whole life as a philosophical loss. The question *How should one act?* divorces one's deeds from oneself in a way that is alienating. Our morality fails to be integrated into our lives; it exists out there, apart from the rest of our existence. If a person is forced to ask about how to act without at the same time seeing the answer to that question as being related to one's particular life, then one's relation to morality becomes fissured. We need to return, these philosophers suggest, to the ancient question, to allow it to renew its hold on us so that once again we may be addressed by philosophy in the space in which we live.

Other philosophers defend the emergence of the modern question as an advance upon the ancient one. Narrowing the focus of the question from lives to action corresponds to a widening of the realm of freedom to choose the life one would like to create. Philosophy should not legislate over the course of one's life; it should not determine the shape it should take, or even whether a life should have a coherent shape. If the rise of individualism and the decline of inequality are to have a meaning for our lives, it is that we can now determine (within the limits prescribed by the answer to the question of *how one should act*) the course and direction of our lives. Each of us must answer to the obligations laid out before him or her; beyond that, philosophy has no business legislating who we ought to be or ought to become. That is our private concern.

In the Continental tradition in philosophy, the modern question gave rise to a third question, one with which we continue to grapple today. Its roots are found scattered throughout the nineteenth century, but nowhere are they given as much nourishment as in the thought of Nietzsche. For Nietzsche, the central event of the late nineteenth century is the death of God. However this death might have occurred (Nietzsche offers different accounts at different points in his work), the implication is profound for human life. Those before Nietzsche who have asked the question of how one should act, almost to a philosopher, have found the answer anchored in a transcendent being, in God. It is a God outside this world that assures us of our obligations within it. The death of God, then, is not merely the demise of a certain theological existence; it is the vanishing of the transcendence in which our morality is grounded. With Nietzsche, not only is there no cosmological order in which to anchor the meaning of our lives, there is also no transcendent set of standards by which to guide our actions. We lack the means we have relied upon to answer the question of how we should act.

We might try to discover other resources that offer guidance in addressing the question of how we should act, resources that are grounded in our own world rather than in a transcendent one. Some philosophers, mostly in the analytic tradition, have taken this route. Nietzsche does not. He is uninterested in the question of how we ought to act; for him, the question is merely a remnant of the period before the death of God. It is an archaism, a bit of nostalgia.

The death of God offers us a new question, one that jettisons the concern with both cosmic roles and individual obligations: *How might one live?*

In Nietzsche's hands, this new question becomes a challenge, a gauntlet thrown at the feet of those whose lives are too narrow. What the long history of asking the questions of how should one live and how should one act has bequeathed us are sad small creatures that can no longer set worthy tasks before us. We have become a species of the petty gesture and the whining complaint. We castigate ourselves with a transcendent (God, the Good) that we can never achieve and whose only function is to reinforce that very castigation. We define ourselves not by what we might create but by what we might hold back from creating; we are our self-denial. In the meantime, what we might be capable of goes not only unanswered but unasked. Those who have the temerity to ask are quickly silenced or removed to the social margins.

It is the death of God and the consequent vanishing of transcendence that reopens the question for us, allowing us to enlarge our lives beyond the limits our history had set for us. Once again we can ask what we might make of ourselves in this world, the world we inhabit. We can stop denying our larger dreams and projects in the name of a transcendence that judges us, and free ourselves instead for what is most noble in our nature.

Much of Continental thought over the course of the twentieth century can be seen as a response to Nietzsche's announcement of the death of God. If God is dead, if we are no longer judged by a transcendence that both diminishes and sustains us, then how might we or how ought we to make our way in the world? How should we think of ourselves? How should we articulate who we are and what we can become?

Jean-Paul Sartre takes up these questions, inaugurating, at least in its contemporary form, the existentialism that forms the immediate legacy of the death of God: "if God does not exist, we find no values or commands to turn to which legitimize our conduct. So, in the bright realm of values, we have no excuse behind us, nor justification before us. We are alone, with no excuses."[3] There is no God. There is no transcendent judge for our acts. We are more alone than the individualism of the modern question could have imagined. We face a future that will be created by decisions that each of us will make with no standard to guide us.

That Sartre, at moments, withdraws from the implications of his own thought is undeniable. In the same pages he announces the vertigo of human freedom, the groundlessness of human choice, he seeks to reintroduce the question of how one ought to act and even to give it a traditional modern answer. But it is too late; the cat is out of the bag. There is no longer a question of how one should live, or how one should act. There is only a question of how one might live.

IV

It is a difficult question, and a frightening one. There is much in us that rebels against confronting it, taking it into our lives and creating ourselves in light of the freedom it offers. It is simpler just to brush our teeth, crawl into our clothing, and burn our days than to ask what we might become. And, as Sartre himself begins to realize in his later years, there is also much outside of our own reticence that militates against our asking the question. The structure of society, the weight of history, the legacy of our language all conspire to keep the question from us, and to keep us from it. Our conformity is not solely a result of individual cowardice; it is built into the world we inhabit.

Several recent French philosophers have forged their philosophical views in the shadow cast by conformity. They have sought to free us

---

[3] Sartre, "Existentialism," p. 23.

from the grip of the structures and forces that produce and reproduce conformity. These philosophers have exposed these structures in our thinking and offered paths to escape them. They have recognized that there is an intimate bond between the ways in which we think about ourselves and our world and the ways in which we construct our lives, and they have sought to address that thinking in order to reach us in our living. In doing so they have nourished the question of how one might live, clearing a space for its asking and for the living that would accompany it.

Deleuze is among these philosophers, but he is by no means the only one. Two others, Michel Foucault and Jacques Derrida, have taken different approaches to the challenge and offered different routes into the question of how one might live. In order to see the peculiarity of Deleuze's own philosophical path, it might be contrasted with Foucault's and Derrida's.

Foucault's works take some of the constraints that seem natural and inevitable to us in order to show that they are, contrary to appearances, historical and contingent. There are aspects of our world that seem to be immune from change. We must conform to the limits they place before us and order our world with those limits in mind. This is more deeply true, and more deeply constraining, when those limits are not merely placed upon us from the outside like barriers but are instead woven into the very fabric of human existence. To attempt to surpass such limits, to seek to live otherwise, would be futile. Far from being a sign of liberation, the project of living otherwise would be a symptom of abnormality. For Foucault, historical study reveals to us that many of these "internal" limits arise not from the constitution of our being but from the politics of our relationships. They are neither natural nor inescapable. "There is an optimism that consists," he writes, "in saying that things couldn't be better. My optimism would consist in saying that so many things can be changed, fragile as they are, more arbitrary than self-evident, more a matter of complex, but temporary, historical circumstances than with inevitable anthropological constraints."[4]

It might seem to be inscribed in the order of things, for instance, that there is a normal course for sexuality to take, and that other courses are deviations from that norm. Homosexuality, bisexuality, promiscuity,

[4] Foucoult, "Practicing Criticism," p. 156.

even female sexual initiative have been in various periods – including our own – accounted as unnatural, as symptoms of a deviance that requires at least intervention and perhaps punishment. To treat homosexuality as a project of pleasure rather than as an expression of abnormality would be to ignore the violation of normal human sexuality that it constitutes. Moreover, to treat a homosexual as something other than a homosexual, to see him or her as defined by something *other than* sexual orientation, is to miss the central element of his or her being. If homosexuality is abnormal, it is an abnormality that swallows up the rest of one's existence; every gesture, every emotion is reducible to the core fact of the homosexuality. That is why it seems so important to intervene. What is at stake is not simply a deviant form of activity; it is a deviant form of life.

But is sexuality naturally or inevitably divided into the normal and the abnormal? Isn't this division rather a historical one, one that serves certain interests and denies others? Foucault argues that it is. Many historians have shown that the concept of homosexuality, for instance, is a recent one, and one that arises not so much from scientific discovery as from psychological categorization. What Foucault adds is the recognition that the central place that sexuality itself occupies in Western culture is a historically determined one. Its importance derives less from a process of neutral intellectual inquiry than from changes in such far-flung practices as the Catholic confessional and population studies, changes which promote the view of desire as constitutive of human beings and of sexuality as the central mode of desire. The result of these changes is to promote both a sexual conformity and, through it, a general social conformity that converge with the economic requirements of capitalism, the political requirements of liberal democracy, and the epistemological requirements of the human sciences such as psychology.

What is true of sexuality is true also for other constraints that the human sciences present to us. "All my analyses are against the idea of universal necessities in human existence. They show the arbitrariness of institutions and show which space of freedom we can still enjoy and how many changes can still be made."[5] Far from being determined by immobile "anthropological constraints," we are instead molded by

5 Foucoult, "Truth, Power, Self: An Interview with Michel Foucault," p. 11.

historical and political forces that can be modified, changed, perhaps even overthrown. The problem – the *philosophical* problem – is that we fail to recognize the historical character of these constraints, and so fail to recognize the freedom before us. We are unable to ask ourselves, in any but the most constricted fashion, how one might live.

If Foucault's approach to the question of how one might live is historical, Jacques Derrida's might be called more nearly linguistic. Derrida shares with Foucault a concern about the constraints our world has placed upon us. Like Foucault, he believes that those constraints arise primarily in the categories by means of which we conceptualize ourselves and our world. Unlike Foucault, however, Derrida finds these constraints to lie in the structure of language. Our oppression is not merely in our historical legacy, but in our very words. Each time we speak, we rely on constraints that haunt our language and that deny us access to addressing the question of how one might live. Because of this, the means to counter those constraints will involve not simply the recognition and overcoming of our historical inheritance; they will involve a nuanced and fragile approach to language itself.

Derrida points out that the project of philosophy consists largely in attempting to build foundations for thought. These foundations work by privileging certain philosophical themes and concepts at the expense of others. Presence is privileged at the expense of absence, identity at the expense of difference, masculinity at the expense of femininity, the literal at the expense of the metaphorical, principles at the expense of sensitivity. In each case of privileging, however, matters turn out to be more complicated than they might seem. It is not merely that it is unjust to privilege one term at the expense of its complement (although there is an injustice there). More deeply, the problem is that the privileged term is, in part, *constituted by the complement.* In philosophical systems that are centered on the concept of presence, that presence cannot be conceived except on the basis of the absence it excludes. Absence does not appear as an other, outside of presence, against which it is understood. It is internal to presence. If we were to put the matter paradoxically, we might say that pure presence can be understood only on the basis of an absence that inhabits it and is partially constitutive of it.

This does not mean that the complements melt into each other, becoming a third category that incorporates the features of each. Rather, they operate in a dynamic relation of distinctness and mutual envelop-ment where the line between them can be neither clearly drawn nor completely erased.

This dynamic, or, as Derrida sometimes calls it, this "economy" of complementary terms – each bleeding into the other without one being able to fix the borders of their meanings – has at least two impli-cations. First, it undercuts the project of philosophical foundational-ism, the project of building a final and unsurpassable foundation for thought. If one cannot fix the meaning of the philosophical terms one uses, if those terms are constantly infiltrated by the terms they are try-ing to exclude, then the foundations themselves will be porous, and in the end unable to hold. It is as though the structure itself will seep into the foundation. This is because, as Derrida recognizes, the project of philosophy is a linguistic one; philosophy is a practice whose medium is words. And, he argues, because of the economy of complementary terms, those words will never be able to be fixed in a way that is solid enough to provide the type of foundation philosophy seeks.

This does not mean that the exclusions – of absence, of the fem-inine, of difference, of metaphor – are overcome. Nor does it mean that the privilegings – of presence, of the masculine, of identity, of the literal – are just. There is still an injustice, a marginalization that must be addressed. Philosophy, as well as everyday thought, still operates by means of these privilegings. They continue to dictate our approach to ourselves and the world. Overcoming this injustice, however, is not a matter of simply inverting the privilege these terms have enjoyed or of trying instead to render them equally privileged. Both approaches would repeat the deeper problem Derrida finds in traditional philoso-phy. They are attempts to fix the terms once and for all rather than to recognize their fluidity. Instead, we must allow the fluidity of terms to remain in play, to negotiate our language in ways that do not suppress but instead allow expression to the economy inherent in it.

If it is language's character to operate by an economy of comple-mentary terms, and if the attempt to deny that economy by fixing the meanings of terms is both futile and unjust, then the approach to language that must be taken is to think and to speak and to write differently. This is primarily a philosophical project, but, like a lot of philosophy, its effects will ripple out into the wider culture.

What bearing does Derrida's approach to philosophy and its language have upon the question of how one might live? By shaking the foundations of the categories through which we conceive ourselves and our world, Derrida opens up new ways of thinking about ourselves, ways that no longer conform to the categories we have inherited. In fact, they do not conform to the idea of categories. When, for instance, we no longer privilege the masculine over the feminine, when we see that these categories bleed into each other, then we are no longer worried about the "essence" of the masculine or the feminine. We become free to borrow from realms that once seemed barred from us. Moreover, we are no longer bound to make those borrowings conform to a pre-given model of what our lives and our world should look like, since the categories within which we would conceive our lives and our world are themselves fluid.

Just as Foucault seeks to reawaken the question of how one might live by showing that what appear to be necessary constraints on our existence are in fact historically contingent, Derrida seeks to reawaken the question by showing that what appear to be strict categories of experience are in fact fluid and interwoven. Beneath these projects there is a deeper bond. Both reject a certain traditional philosophical project that falls under the rubric of *ontology*.

The term *ontology* has several different meanings in philosophy. In the analytic tradition, it means "the study of what there is," either in general or in some specific area. What are the ultimate constituents of the universe? Is everything that exists ultimately physical matter or do such things as numbers or ideas or sets also exist? Or, at a more specific level, what are the constituents of psychology: the mind, behavior, bodies in interaction? Can we reduce psychological accounts of human existence to purely physical ones? These are among the questions pondered by ontology in analytic thought. In Continental thought, ontology has come to mean "the study of being (or Being)." This approach takes its cue from the work of Martin Heidegger, who argues that over the course of Western philosophy, stretching as far back as Plato, the "question of Being" has been forgotten and needs to be recovered. What is being? What is the meaning of being? What is it for something to *be*? These are the driving questions of ontology among Continental thinkers.

There can be a convergence between analytic and Continental approaches to ontology. Both ask about the nature of what there is. But their inflections on this asking are different. Analytic philosophers are interested in the beings of which the universe is constituted. They seek to account for the nature and existence of those beings and their relationships to one another. Continental philosophers often see a question of being that cannot be addressed in terms of constituent beings. Following Heidegger, they see in the attempt to reduce the question of being to that of beings a symptom of an age that is too ready to accept the terms in which science conceives the world.

For their part Derrida and Foucault both reject ontology in the first, analytic, sense.

Foucault rejects any ontology of human being, any account of the ultimate nature of human being. When he says that all of his analyses are against the idea of necessities in human existence, he is refusing to engage in an ontology of the human. What appear to be ontological matters are in reality historical matters parading in ontological garb. We are taught that there are certain norms, tendencies, and orientations that human beings, by virtue of being human, possess. There are specific sexual, psychological, cognitive, and emotional lives that are characteristically human. To fail to live in accordance with these characteristically human lives is to fail to be fully human. It is to be abnormal. The lesson of Foucault's histories is that what is considered characteristically human, and therefore normal, is the product of a politically charged history. Abnormality need not be seen as a violation of the norms of human existence. It can as well be a refusal to conform to the "ontological" requirements of a given historical moment.

Derrida's rejection of ontology occurs not at the level of specific human ontologies but at the level of the terms used to fix any ontology. What vitiates the ontological project in his eyes concerns the language in which an ontology would be articulated. Any ontology is an attempt to give an exhaustive account of what there is, to discover some essential nature at the bottom of things. But if linguistic terms are permeable in the way Derrida thinks, then the very terms in which that nature is articulated will be haunted by terms they are trying to exclude. There is no path to an account of an essential nature that would not be permeated by the nonessential as an inextricable aspect.

The project of constructing an ontology that separates what is from what is not is doomed by the economy of the terms it uses.

Whether Foucault or Derrida reject ontology in the second, Continental, sense is a more difficult question. Foucault is largely uninterested in the question of being. Derrida, by contrast, sees himself as following through on many of Heidegger's concerns.[6] What they would certainly reject, however, would be any approach to the question of being by means of an account that says, ultimately, what there is. For both Foucault and Derrida any approach to the question of being that goes by means of an account of an unchanging, pure nature or essence is misguided, for either historical or linguistic reasons. Misguided, and worse than misguided: harmful. To address the question of being by means of an account of what there is would seem to constrain human behavior to a narrow conformity. It would fail to keep alive the question of how one might live.

And that is the point at which they diverge from Deleuze, who approaches the question of how one might live not by abandoning ontology, but by embracing it.

V

Deleuze's works are steeped in ontology. Each work posits a new group of fundamental entities or reworks entities from previous works into a new context. To read Deleuze is to be introduced into a world of proliferating beings and new forms of life. These beings and forms of life are not a part of our everyday experience. Nevertheless they inhere in the fabric of our existence.

While Foucault and Derrida seek to unravel the pretensions of ontology as a study of what there is, Deleuze revels in ontological creation and analysis. While Foucault and Derrida find ontology to be a threat to asking how one might live, Deleuze finds ontology to be the very route one must take in order to ask about it adequately. While Foucault and Derrida offer alternatives to the traditional philosophical project of ontology, Deleuze drives that project to its limit, a limit at which he

---

[6] Deconstruction is in many ways a continuation of Heidegger's *Destruktion* of traditional philosophy, and *différance* may be read as an approach to Heidegger's ontic-ontological difference.

finds the question of how one might live to be raised afresh and ready to offer surprising answers.

By embracing ontology as the study of what there is Deleuze does not only go against the anti-ontological trend of much of twentieth-century philosophy. His work also cuts against the grain of those who have approached the question of how one might live. For Deleuze's predecessors and contemporaries, breathing life into that question requires abandoning what had been considered ontologically necessary, eliminating the search for entities that constrain us to asking questions less radical than that of how one might live. For Nietzsche the question of how one might live is opened up by the death of God, that is, the loss of any constraining ontological transcendence. For Sartre existentialism involves a recognition that nothing makes us be what we are, that we are free to create ourselves without an essential ontological nature that dictates the inescapable course of our lives. For Foucault the identities offered to us by our history must be recognized as contingent rather than necessary, as passing phenomena rather than ontological requirements. Only then will we be able to ask the question of how one might live without already constricting the answer to the conformity that forms the ether of our world. Finally, for Derrida the rigid ontologies of traditional philosophy veil the fluidity of their terms, a fluidity that undercuts the very project of saying what there is and what there is not. That fluidity must be unveiled if we are to reopen the question of how one might live.

It would seem that if one hopes to address the question of how one might live in a way that does not reinforce a tired conformity, then ontology – at least inasmuch as it is the study of what there is – is the problem rather than the solution.

Is this the inescapable fate of ontology? Must it disappear from the field of philosophical reflection if our task is to ask the question of how one might live without falling back either into concerns about how one should act or how one ought to live or into an unquestioning conformism?

Deleuze denies this in his work. He denies it by creating an ontology, or rather a series of ontologies, that challenge two assumptions underlying the rejection of an ontological approach to the question. The first assumption is that ontology involves discovery rather than creation. What other thinkers who have been grasped by the question of how one might live have assumed is that ontology is an attempt to *discover* the nature of the universe's fundamental entities. Why must one see ontology as a matter of discovery, however, as opposed to *creation?* It is true that philosophers who engage in ontology almost universally see themselves as attempting to glean the essential character of what there is. They assume that the study of what there is consists of accounting in the most adequate fashion for the nature of what exists. And it is precisely this assumption that has worried those who ask the question of how one might live. Such accounting seems always to be a reduction of possibilities, a narrowing of perspective that ends up impoverishing the universe. A universe composed solely of physical entities in more or less predictable relationships with one another, a humanity characterized by narrow norms of behavior, a realm of entities rigidly demarcated from one another: these are worlds that constrict rather than widen the question of how one might live.

Is this how ontology must be done? Are we excluded from approaching ontology another way? Suppose we were to see the study of what there is as a creation rather than a discovery, or, better, as a project where the distinction between creation and discovery is no longer relevant. Suppose that ontology were not a project of seeking to grasp what there is in the most accurate way. Suppose instead ontology were to construct frameworks that, while not simply matters of fiction, were not simply matters of explanation either. Is it not possible to invert the traditional relationship, so that the question of how one might live is no longer based upon the question of what there is but vice versa? In other words, could one not create an ontology whose purpose is to open the question of how one might live to new vistas? Nietzsche, Sartre, Foucault, and Derrida have shown the constrictions that arise when the question of how one might live must answer to ontology. Deleuze suggests that it is possible to move in the opposite direction, to create an ontology that answers to the question of how one might live rather than dictating its limits.

Such an ontology would not only invert the traditional relationship between creation and discovery. It would also invert the traditional relationship between identity and difference. This is the second assumption about ontology that Deleuze challenges. It is intertwined with the first one.

If ontology is a project solely of discovery, its point is to articulate the nature or essence of what is. It is to offer us the *identity* of what is. An identity requires conceptual stability. In order for something to have an identity, it must have characteristics that can be *identified* over time. Those characteristics do not need to be stable. The stability needs to be possessed only by the concepts that identify them. Certain kinds of instabilities might be identified, and might be part of the identity of what is. If Freud is correct in his view of human development, tensions between one's present relationships and one's earlier parental relationships are of the nature of human being. No particular way of resolving these tensions is essential to human unfolding; the identity of human beings, however, is caught in the web of those tensions and the instabilities that emerge from them. And the character of the tensions themselves can be identified. That character can be captured in words that possess conceptual stability, words like *Oedipus complex* and *transfer*.

Without conceptual stability there can be no discovery of the kind ontology has always sought. Unless we can articulate what there is in words that actually identify it, our discoveries slip through our conceptual grasp. We are left with chaos, with a realm that defies our understanding, that resists our attempt to *say* what there is and to *say* what it is like. There is no identity here, because what there is cannot be identified in a way that allows us to engage in ontology.

In their different ways, Nietzsche and Sartre and Foucault and Derrida argue that there are no ontological identities to be discovered, because what looks like a stable identity is not. Particular identities have become sedimented in our philosophical views not because they reflect the ways things really are but because our history or our fears or our language has placed them there. Ontology, far from being an engagement with what is, denies the shifting character of reality or the porous quality of our language. Since it is a project of discovery, ontology requires identity; because it does so it is a philosophical failure.

According to Deleuze, the failure of ontology to discover identifiable entities does not spell the end of ontology, the "death of philosophy" as some writers would have it. This failure is, in fact, the beginning of ontology. We can engage in ontology, the only kind of ontology worth doing – ontology that responds to the question of how one might live – when we cease to see it as a project of identity. We begin ontology when we abandon the search for conceptual stability and begin to see what there is in terms of difference rather than identity: "difference is behind everything, but behind difference there is nothing."[7]

To see being as difference is at once to refuse to philosophize in terms of identities and to jettison the project of ontology as discovery. It is not, however, to resort to fiction. The abandonment of discovery is not an announcement that philosophy has given the field over to novel writing. We need not posit two stable concepts – discovery and creation – and conclude that since philosophy is not solely the first then it is nothing more than the second. Just as fiction writers are constrained by the characters they create, by the situations those characters find themselves in, and by the flow of the narrative itself, philosophy is constrained, but in different ways.

What is philosophy? It is "the art of forming, inventing, and fabricating concepts."[8] A concept is not a fiction, but neither is it a discovery. A concept is a way of addressing the difference that lies beneath the identities we experience. It is a way of articulating the hidden virtual reality out of which the actually experienced reality emerges. In Deleuze's hands, philosophy does not seek to offer a coherent framework from within which we can see ourselves and our world whole. It does not put everything in its place. It does not tell us who we are or what we ought to do. Philosophy does not settle things. It disturbs them. Philosophy disturbs by moving beneath the stable world of identities to a world of difference that at once produces those identities and shows them to be little more than the froth of what there is. And it does this by creating concepts. Concepts reach beneath the identities our world presents to us in order to touch upon the world of difference that both constitutes and disrupts those identities.

A concept does not stand alone. It links up with other concepts, coexists with them on a "plane of immanence" that allows different concepts to resonate together in a multitude of ways. "It is the plane that secures conceptual linkages with ever increasing connections, and it is concepts that secure the populating of the plane on an always renewed and variable curve."[9] Together, concepts and the plane of

7 Deleuze, *Difference and Repetition*, p. 57.

8 Deleuze and Guattari, *What Is Philosophy?*, p. 2.

9 Deleuze and Guattari, *What Is Philosophy?*, p. 37.

immanence give voice to the difference that is behind everything and behind which there is nothing.

How is this possible? How can a concept capture something that is not an identity but instead lies beneath it and within it? Although we have yet only begun to approach the difference Deleuze speaks of, we can already recognize that it cannot be given an identity. Difference is not identified. What is the relationship between a concept or a philosophical perspective consisting in concepts on a plane and the difference it articulates? In traditional ontology, concepts *identify* what there is. What can a concept do with that which cannot be identified?

Concepts do not identify difference, they *palpate* it. When doctors seek to understand a lesion they cannot see, they palpate the body. They create a zone of touch where the sense of the lesion can emerge without its being directly experienced. They use their fingers to create an understanding where direct identification is impossible. This sense or understanding is not an emotional one. It is not an effect. (For Deleuze, art is the realm of effects; philosophy is the realm of concepts.) We might say that palpation "gives voice" to the lesion. It allows the lesion to speak: not in its own words, for it has none, but in a voice that will at least not be confused with something it is not.

Palpation is not a traditional philosophical activity. It does not seek to comprehend, if by comprehension we mean bringing within our intellectual control. Traditional ontology would like to match its concepts to what there is, to map what there is by means of concepts that are adequate to it. Adequacy requires truth, conceptual stability, and in the end identity. But if it is difference rather than identity we seek, and the interesting and remarkable rather than the true, then it is palpation rather than comprehension we require.

If a doctor palpates something that cannot be directly perceived, philosophy palpates something that cannot be directly comprehended. It palpates something that eludes our theoretical grasp, something that – as we will see in a moment – eludes our knowledge.

Concepts palpate difference, and by doing so they give voice to it. It is a strange voice, eerie and perturbing. It is not the voice of the pop singer or the news anchor. Nor is it the voice of the legislator or the professor. The voice of difference arises from a place that is at once distant and intimate, that is both of us and not of us. And the creation of concepts, which in Deleuze's view is the only significant endeavor in which philosophy can engage, seeks to palpate and give voice to this difference that disrupts all projects of identification. Philosophy is ontology; it speaks of what there is. But what there is cannot be identified. Or better, what can be identified is only a single manifestation, a single actualization, of what there is. What there is is difference: a difference that is not simply the distinction between two identities (which would subordinate difference to identity) or the negation of one of them (which would think of difference only negatively). What there is is a difference in itself, a pure difference that forms the soil for all identities, all distinctions, and all negations. The task of philosophy is to create concepts for difference.

Deleuze often uses the word *thought* to refer to philosophy that takes its task seriously.[10] He distinguishes thought from knowledge. Knowledge is the recognition and understanding of identities. When we know something we have a cognitive grasp of its identity. Most philosophers have taken the project of philosophy to be that of knowledge. Philosophers in the analytic tradition have surely done so. In modeling their work on that of the sciences or mathematics, they have sought to gain knowledge in areas not traditionally associated with those fields, for instance in the nature of knowledge or of language. (However, as Deleuze argues, there are surprises that both mathematics and science hold in store for those who see them as exemplary fields of knowledge. It will be seen in Chapter 3 of this book that there is more of what Deleuze calls *thought* going on in them than is often realized.) Thought, by contrast, does not identify and so does not give us knowledge. It moves beyond what is known to the difference beneath, behind, and within it. And, since difference outruns thought, thought can only palpate a difference that lies beyond its grasp. There is always more to think. There is always more philosophy to be done.

Does this mean that philosophy, when it is done properly as thought rather than as knowledge, offers us fictions? Does knowledge concern itself with discovery, and thought (in Deleuze's sense) with creation? Have we not returned to the distinction we were just trying to erase between what can be found and what is made up?

We do so only if we must believe that difference is a fiction. But we are not forced to believe that. Difference is no more a creation

---

[10] See, for example, his pages on thinking in Michel Foucault in his *Foucault*, pp. 116–19.

than it is a discovery. Concepts of difference are not like fictional characters. They do not ask us to suspend belief. But neither do they ask us to believe. Assent or denial are not the responses concepts seek. "Philosophy does not consist in knowing and is not inspired by truth. Rather, it is categories like Interesting, Remarkable, or Important that determine success or failure."[11] The destiny of philosophical concepts and philosophical positions lie not with the truth or falsity of their claims but with the vistas for thinking and living they open up for us. If knowledge seeks to answer the question, "What can we know that we did not know before?" philosophy is motivated by a different query: "How can we see what we did not see before?"

"How?" is not simply a what, since what we see and how we see it are, in philosophy, inseparable. Philosophical concepts and the philosophical views upon which they are built offer us not merely something to be seen – difference – but also a way of seeing it. That way of doing philosophy is not interested in whether what is seen really exists: Is there difference, really? Nor does it, like fiction, assume that there is no such thing as difference, really, but that if we make it up we can create new and interesting worlds. Philosophy is not inspired by truth, but it is not inspired by fiction either. Instead, philosophy creates a way of seeing this world in which we live that disturbs the verities we are presented with, that opens up new ways of seeing and of conceiving this world that, rather than true or false, are interesting, remarkable, or important. "Thinking," Deleuze writes of Nietzsche, "would then mean *discovering, inventing, new possibilities of life*."[12]

Deleuze remarks in one of his books that "Every time someone puts an objection to me, I want to say: 'OK, OK, let's go on to something else.' "[13] This is not because he does not want to be faced with any shortcomings his work might have; it is because philosophy, as he does it, is not about argument. It is not about seeking the truth beneath divergent opinions. Philosophy is about ontology, and ontology is about concepts of difference, and concepts of difference are not seeking to articulate a truth; they are creating a perspective on what there is. What motivates this perspective is the question of how one might live.

---

[11] Deleuze and Guattari, *What Is Philosophy?*, p. 82.
[12] Deleuze *Nietzsche and Philosophy*, p. 101.
[13] Deleuze and Parnet, *Dialogues*, p. 1.

Foucault and Derrida teach us that if we think of our lives solely in terms of what appears to us, and if we think of what appears to us as exhausting our possibilities, we are already hedged in, already committed to conformism. Their response is to say that we ought to stop thinking in terms of ontology, at least in the analytic sense, because ontology teaches us that what appears to us is natural and inevitable. Things cannot be otherwise. Deleuze agrees with their diagnosis, but not with their cure. If the question is how might one live, the way to approach it is with another ontology, one that offers possibilities as yet undreamed of, one whose soil is far richer than those plants to which it has yet given rise.

VI

Deleuze approaches the question of how one might live as a complex one. It is not simply a question of how we human beings might go about creating our lives, of what we might decide to make ourselves into. We might not want to think of the question that way at all. There are several ways to interpret what is being asked with the question of how might one live. That it is a question addressing the creation of human lives is only one of those interpretations. Deleuze is interested in at least two others.

The question might also be interpreted as asking for a speculation of what life might be about, how it is that living happens. *How might one live?* might mean something like, "What might living consist in?" What is being asked for here is not so much an accounting of our future possibilities as a perspective on what it is to be alive. To be sure, our future possibilities are not divorced from what our living consists in. What worries the thinkers we have discussed is precisely that a narrow view of what living consists in needlessly constrains our conception of future possibilities. The two are related. But they are not the same question. In approaching ontology, Deleuze directs his attention far more to the question of what living might consist in than to the question of our future possibilities. It is our future possibilities that everywhere concern him. But he addresses them by offering an ontology adequate to them. He tells us what our living consists in in order that each of us might better ask ourselves about our future possibilities.

To ask what living consists in, as an ontological matter, is not the same thing as asking about it as a biological one. The answer will not be given in terms of carbon; it will be given in terms of difference. For Deleuze, living consists in difference and its actualization. Difference is not a thing, it is a process. It unfolds – or better, it is an unfolding (and a folding, and a refolding). It is alive. Not with cells or with respiration, but with vitality. To ask what living consists in is to ask about this vitality at the heart of things.

Another way of interpreting the question is concerned less with the word *living* than with the word *one*. So far we have taken the word *one* to mean person. We need not. If living is a matter of the unfolding of a vital difference, then the one that lives can be either less or more or other than a person. It can be a mouth, a gesture, a style, a relationship. It can be a group or an epoch. To embed the concept of living in people is to commit the error of humanism, the error of believing that the proper perspective for understanding the world is centered on the viewpoint of the human subject. Deleuze tries to pry us away from humanism by focusing on a difference that need not be human difference and a one that need not be a person. I can be the one who lives, but so can my hand or my relationship with my wife or the way my body navigates through a crowded room.

There is no reason to privilege the life of the subject above other lives. Nor is there any reason to reject it. It is one perspective on difference, one way of getting a conceptual hold of it. There are others, neither more nor less adequate. Or, rather their adequacy depends on how they contribute to living. The mistake all along was to believe that there was only one, and that it was the human one.

The question of how one might live, then, is not simply a question of how a human being might go about creating his or her future. It is that, too. But it is not merely that. As a question of ontology, it concerns the creation of concepts of difference that allow us to consider living at different levels. Among these levels we may find a variety of understandings of ourselves, and this variety of understandings may open up a variety of futures to be lived. This multiplicity and diffusion of concepts and perspectives is not a difficulty for Deleuze's philosophy. It is the point.

The philosopher John Rajchman may have put it best: "In a modern world of stupefying banality, routine, cliché, mechanical reproduction or automatism, the problem is to extract a singular image, a vital, multiple way of thinking and saying, not a substitute theology."[14] In Chapter 5 we will return to this. But it can already be glimpsed that Deleuze's ontology does not give us a prescription for living. In approaching the question of how one might live, Deleuze does not offer us a simple formula: Live thus. If his ontology is concerned with difference, then the future must be concerned with experimentation. We can discover our possibilities – my possibilities, but also the possibilities of my hand, my relationships, the groups in which I participate, the style of an artistic movement – by probing difference, seeing what new foldings, unfoldings, and refoldings it is capable of. "This is how it should be done: Lodge yourself on a stratum, experiment with the opportunities it offers, find an advantageous place on it, find potential movements of deterritorialization, possible lines of flight, experience them, produce flow conjunctions here and there, try out continuums of intensities segment by segment, have a small plot of new land at all times."[15]

We need not conform. Indeed, if our lives are to be interesting ones, capable of new feelings, new pleasures, new thoughts and experiences, we must not conform. Deleuze offers us a radically different way to approach living, and an attractive one, as long as we are willing to ask anew what it is to be *us* and what it is to be *living*. As long as we are willing to accept that ontology does not offer answers but rather ways to approach the question of living. As long as we turn to his work not to settle old questions or old scores but instead to become unsettled. In short, as long as we are willing to do philosophy.

[14] Rajchman, *The Deleuze Connections*, p. 125.
[15] Deleuze and Guattari, *A Thousand Plateaus*, p. 161.

2

Spinoza, Bergson, Nietzsche

The Holy Trinity

I

Deleuze and Guattari write, "Spinoza is the Christ of philosophers, and the greatest philosophers are hardly more than apostles who distance themselves or draw near this mystery."[1] If Spinoza is the Christ among Deleuze's philosophers, then Bergson is the Father, and Nietzsche the Holy Ghost. Spinoza offers us immanence, difference made flesh. Bergson offers us the temporality of duration, without which immanence cannot be born. And the spirit of Nietzsche, of the active and the creative affirmation of difference without recoupment into some form of identity, pervades the entire project.

Deleuze writes of other thinkers. There are books on Hume, Kant, Proust, Sacher-Masoch, Kafka, Foucault, and Leibniz. There are appeals to Lucretius, Scotus, and Heidegger, allusions to Melville, Henry Miller, Michel Tournier, Pierre Klossowski, Joyce, and scientific references to Monod and Prigogine. But in the end, there are three who stand above the others. It is they who provide the motivation and the framework for the ontologies Deleuze constructs over the course of his many writings. Immanence, duration, affirmation: Spinoza, Bergson, Nietzsche. These are the parameters of an ontology of difference.

---

[1] Deleuze and Guattari, *What Is Philosophy?*, p. 60.

II

Immanence is the first requirement of an ontology of difference. Philosophy cannot admit transcendence without lapsing into inadequate concepts, concepts of identity, concepts that ultimately lead us to conformism. "We must draw up a list of... illusions and take their measure, just as Nietzsche, following Spinoza, listed the 'four great errors.' But the list is infinite. First of all there is the *illusion of transcendence*, which, perhaps, comes before all the others."[2]

Transcendence freezes living, makes it coagulate and lose its flow; it seeks to capture the vital difference that outruns all thought and submit it to the judgment of a single perspective, a perspective that stands outside difference and gathers it into manageable categories. Transcendence substitutes knowledge for thought.

That which transcends stands outside or above. It is beyond. The God of the Judeo-Christian tradition is the primary example. God transcends. He transcends the world, but also transcends human experience. He is beyond anything we can conceive of him. (This transcendence, it seems, does not preclude God from giving special messages to his self-elected representatives about what he wants, but that is another matter – a matter of politics.) In the history of philosophy, a history dominated by the motif of transcendence, it is the transcendence of God that forms the longest legacy. But it is not the only one.

Before there is God there are the Platonic Forms. The Forms stand outside human experience; they transcend the world, not only the experienced world but the world itself. (Difference, it turns out, transcends the *experienced* world but does not transcend the world itself. It is transcendent to our knowledge, but not to that which gives knowledge.) The role of the philosopher is to seek to understand the Forms. The philosopher seeks cognitive participation in them, wanting to grasp intellectually their nature and, ultimately, to mold the world in their likeness. The latter task belongs to the philosopher king: to apply the lessons of transcendence to this world. Philosophers are required as rulers for a just society because there is a transcendence to be understood and learned from. That is the lesson of the allegory of the cave in Plato's *Republic*.

---

[2] Deleuze and Guattari, *What Is Philosophy?*, p. 49.

Before the philosopher's role becomes that of understanding the transcending God and our relationship to that God, then, it is to understand the transcending Forms and our participation in them. And after God there is human subjectivity.

Human subjectivity does not immediately replace God. Descartes' ambivalence between the power of the cogito and the power of God reflects the difficult birth of the human subject. Descartes doubts everything that can be doubted, leaving intact only the human subject that doubts. But the subject is not yet capable of constructing a world; that moment awaits the arrival of Berkeley and then Kant. For Descartes, the human subject requires assistance, an assistance that can be provided only by God. So the seeds of God are built into the subjectivity to which doubt has reduced Descartes, but God's being also transcends that subjectivity. Epistemologically, the human subject is first: it is the seat of knowledge. Ontologically, however, the subject follows in God's wake, since God both grants and guarantees the experience of the subject.

This is a dual transcendence, of subjectivity from the world and of God from both the subject and the world. The first transcendence gives birth to the mind-body problem: if the mind transcends the body, then what is their relationship? The second transcendence carries on the ancient and medieval tradition of the transcendence of God.

In time, the first transcendence displaces the second one. The human subject transcends the material world, constituting it and giving it form. From Kant to Sartre, philosophy is in thrall to a human subjectivity that abandons God not by overthrowing transcendence but by gradually usurping God's place in it. The primacy of the human subject is not a turn to immanence, not an immersion in the world, but transcendence carried on by other means.

A philosophy of transcendence, whether of Forms or of God or of the human subject, requires two commitments and is haunted by a single question. The first commitment is to the existence of two ontological substances, two types of being. If God transcends the world, it cannot be made of the same substance as the world. The world's substance is finite, changeable, even at its best intellectually limited. God is infinite, unchanging, and omniscient. If it were otherwise, there would be no sense to the idea of God's transcendence. God might be elsewhere in space and time, but he would not be *beyond*.

So it is with human subjectivity. There is a material world and a mental one. The material world is physical, spatially limited, inert. The mental world is less limited (although more limited than God), active, and constituting of the material world. This does not mean that the mental world actually creates the material world. Constitution does not imply creation. It is not as though there were only mental substance and then, by some miracle, physical substance was created from it. What is created is not the *material* but the *world*. The *what it is* of the material world, its character, is constituted by the mental world, woven from the material world's inert threads into a meaningful complex. It is only a mind that can make a world. Without it there is simply silence.

Transcendence requires the existence of at least two ontological substances. That is its first commitment. It also requires that one of those substances be superior to the other. Superior in power, and superior in value as well. The Forms, God, and the human subject are all superior to the worlds they transcend. The Forms constitute the true nature of the degraded copies that are found in the world. Deleuze writes of Plato's thought that "The foundation [the Forms] is that which possesses something in a primary way; it relinquishes it to be participated in, giving it to the suitor, who possesses only secondarily and insofar as he has been able to pass the test of the foundation."[3]

God is omnipotent, omniscient, and all good. There would be no problem of evil were God not superior to the world he creates and sustains.

The human subject creates a world from the inert material it is presented with. If God said, "Let there be light," and there was light, then without the human subject it would not be light. It would just be there, without name or form, performing no function except to sustain a mute world of animality.

In each case – the Forms, God, the human subject – the constituting power is valued more highly than that which it constitutes. The superior power is not a foreign occupying force, colonizing the world it transcends. It is not an invader, unwanted, corrupting an original purity. If anything it is the opposite. The transcending power brings

3 Deleuze, *The Logic of Sense*, p. 255.

the transcended world into full flower, liberating it from the prison of its incapacity, its impotence. Transcendence does not corrupt; it completes. It offers significance to a substance that would otherwise be nothing more than a wound in space and time. That is why it is a moral duty to seek the Forms or to follow God, why it is that human subjectivity is the highest form of (finite) being.

All of this follows from the commitment to transcendence. It does not follow as a matter of pure logic. It is not contradictory to say that the transcending substance is of the same type as the transcended substance, or that it is not superior. Rather, it follows as a matter of the role of transcendence in the history of philosophy.

The first commitment is simply understood. If there were two substances of the same type then they would either interact and become one substance or they would not interact and would instead form two separate universes. But for philosophy there has only been one universe to be explained: our universe. So if there are two substances, one transcending the other, they must be different in character. However, although different in character, the two substances must interact. If they did not interact, once again there would be two different universes. The two universes would be universes of different substances rather than the same substance. But they would nevertheless be two universes.

In order for there to be transcendence, then, in a universe that we recognize as our own, there must be two different interacting substances.

Regarding the second commitment, it is hardly a logical requirement that the interaction between the two substances privilege one of them, either in power or in value. One can imagine a transcendence where both substances were equal. However, the point of transcendence has always been to reach *beyond* this world. Why reach beyond it if what is to be grasped is not superior in power or value to what is already here? Nietzsche understood this as the ascetic undercurrent of much of human history, especially religious history. "The idea at issue in this struggle is the *value* which the ascetic priests ascribe to our life: they juxtapose this life (along with what belongs to it, 'nature', 'world', the whole sphere of becoming and the ephemeral) to a completely different form of existence, which it opposes and excludes, *unless* it somehow turns itself against itself, *denies itself.*"[4] What transcends must be superior to what exists before us, or else there would be no point in our seeking it.

This is as true of human subjectivity as it is of God or the Forms. In the Judeo-Christian tradition, subjectivity is bound to the spirit, which resists the temptations of the flesh. And even when it pries itself apart from its moorings in religion, the human subject as active and constituting takes on the powers formerly associated with God.

With these last considerations we can begin to glimpse the role of transcendence. It is to allow the universe to be explained in such a way as to privilege one substance at the expense of another, to preserve the superiority of certain characteristics and to denigrate others. What is to be recognized as superior is not of this world: the infinite, the nonphysical, the unlimited, and the unity of a self-identity. But what is of more moment for Deleuze's thought is what is to be denigrated: the physical, the chaotic, that which resists identity. Only that which submits to participation in the identity of the Forms, or that which follows the narrow dictates of God, or that which conforms to the conceptual categories of human thought is to be admitted into the arena of the acceptable. Physicality, chaos, difference that cannot be subsumed into categories of identity: all these must deny themselves if they would seek to be recognized in the privileged company of the superior substance.

The commitments of transcendence, to two substances and to a privileging of one of them, lead us to the questions all philosophies of transcendence must face. How does the interaction between the two substances occur? If there are two substances of different types, what is the means of communication between the two?

It is a question without an obvious answer. Those who have held the mind to be distinct from the human body have been challenged to discover the means of their interaction. Descartes' answer was that they interacted in the pineal gland.[5] But this is not an answer. It is only geography. It tells us where the interaction takes place. What we need to know, however, is how it happens.

4 Nietzsche, *On the Genealogy of Morals*, p. 96.
5 See further, Descartes, *The Passions of the Soul.*

III

How does the participation by physical substances in the forms occur? How does God relate to his creatures? How do mental thoughts create movements in the body?

Deleuze does not worry about these questions. He does not like to argue. He does not like to harp on weaknesses in a philosopher's work. He would rather change the subject. *"Every time someone puts an objection to me I want to say: 'OK, OK, let's go on to something else.'"* When he discusses Plato, he is not concerned that there may be a difficulty in accounting for the participation in the Forms. Instead, he is fascinated by something else: that it is Plato himself who offers a way to undercut transcendence. Plato's concern is to distinguish the real copies of a given form from the pretenders, the simulacra. He wants to discover those copies that are worthy of participation, those that possess an actual resemblance to their proper Form, and so must distinguish them from those copies that merely pretend to resemble but in actuality are different from it. He must distinguish the real participants from the false pretenders. It is with the concept of the simulacrum that Plato himself begins to point the way out of Platonic transcendence. "Plato discovers, in the flash of an instant, that the simulacrum is not simply a false copy, but that it places in question the very notations of copy and model. . . . Was it not Plato himself who pointed out the direction for the reversal of Platonism?"[6]

Deleuze is also not concerned about the conceptual difficulties of the relationship between God and his creatures or the mind and the body. Spinoza is. His major arguments at the outset of the first part of the *Ethics* aim at refuting the claim that there can be more than one substance, in order to be able to conclude in proposition 14: *"There can be, or be conceived, no other substance but God. "*[7] His major arguments in the beginning of the second part of *Ethics'* aim at refuting the ontological distinction between mind and body, in order to be able to conclude in proposition 7: *"The order and connection of ideas is the same as the order and connection of things,"* with its scholium, "thinking substance and extended substance are one and the same substance, comprehended

---

[6] Deleuze, *The Logic of Sense*, p. 256.
[7] Spinoza, *The Ethics and Selected Letters*, p. 39.

now under this attribute, now under that."[8] What concerns Deleuze is not what Spinoza criticizes but the model of immanence he constructs in its stead. It is not that Spinoza has detailed the difficulties of transcendence that fascinates Deleuze. Rather, it is that Spinoza has successfully changed the subject, gone on to something else. He has done so by employing a concept that allows thinking to abandon transcendence: the concept of expression.

In Spinoza's time the concepts of substance, attributes, and modes are the standard fare of philosophy. Attributes are the characteristics or essences of substance, modes their concrete appearance in reality. An attribute of mental substance is that it thinks; a mode is a specific thought. An attribute of physical substance is that it is extended. My body is one of its modes. God's attributes are omniscience, omnipotence, etc.: it has no modes. The relationship between substance and mode, particularly the divine substance of God, is one of either creation or emanation.

In creation, God exercises his omnipotence in order to put something in place that did not exist before. The Genesis story of the creation of the physical universe is usually interpreted in this way. There was nothing but God, until God brought the universe into being. The usual way of thinking about the relationship between what exists and God is along the lines of creation. Emanation is like creation in that there remains a distinction between the creator and the created. The difference is that what is created comes from the substance of the creator, emanates from it. If I were an artist who was able not only to mold the material before me but also to will the very material to appear, I would be engaging in creation. If my art were instead torn from my flesh, I would be engaged in emanation.

Deleuze points out that emanation, unlike creation, has an affinity with expression: "*they produce while remaining in themselves.*"[9] Both emanation and expression see substance as being of a single type, since what appears in the creation is of the same stuff as the creator. But the similarity ends there. In emanation, what is created is distinct from the creator. Moreover, the creator remains privileged in regard to its creation. "Emanation thus serves as the principle

---

[8] Spinoza, *The Ethics and Selected Letters*, pp. 66–7.
[9] Deleuze, *Expressionism in Philosophy: Spinoza*, p. 171.

of a universe rendered hierarchical...each term is as it were the
image of the superior term that precedes it, and is defined by the
degree of distance that separates it from the first cause or the first
principle."[10]

Emanation, like creation, preserves the two commitments of a philosophy of transcendence: the existence of two substances and the
superiority of one of those substances: "the themes of creation or
emanation cannot do without a minimal transcendence, which bars
'expressionism' from proceeding all the way to the immanence it implies."[11] The difference between "expressionism" in the quoted passage and expressionism as Deleuze intends it lies in the turn toward
immanence.

That both creation and emanation retain a commitment to transcendence is no accident. There is a religious necessity pushing ontology into the arms of transcendence. Without transcendence, what
do we make of God? In what sense is God superior to the creatures of
this world, if not by being *beyond* them? God cannot compel us, cannot
command our devotion, unless he transcends the boundaries of our
world. Just as for Plato the Forms take their aura of superiority in being
beyond the world of shadows that we inhabit, for the Judeo-Christian
tradition God finds his luster in transcending the parameters of our
universe. Spinoza is a heretic, but his heresy lies not in pantheism but
in the denial of transcendence and in the construction of an ontology of immanence. It was for this that the Christ of philosophers was
crucified.

What is an ontology of immanence? Its first requirement is the univocity of being: "expressive immanence cannot be sustained unless it
is accompanied by a thoroughgoing conception of univocity, a thoroughgoing affirmation of univocal Being."[12] The substance of being
is one and indivisible. There are no distinctions to be made into different substances, different layers of substance, different types of substance, or different levels of substance. All hierarchy and division is
banished from ontology. The term "being" (or "Being") is said in one
and the same sense of everything of which it is said. Without univocity,

[10] Deleuze, *Expressionism in Philosophy: Spinoza*, p. 173.
[11] Deleuze, *Expressionism in Philosophy: Spinoza*, p. 180.
[12] Deleuze, *Expressionism in Philosophy: Spinoza*, p. 178.

transcendence will inevitably return to haunt the construction of any ontology.

Emanation is an example of the haunting of ontology by transcendence. One starts with a single substance, God. He is univocal. There are no distinctions among its substance. One can imagine that it could emanate itself and yet remain univocal. That would be expressionism. In the medieval tradition in which the concept of emanation arises, however, that is not what happens. In order to preserve the transcendence of God, emanation introduces the twofold distinction into substance: God is different from what is emanated, and higher. No matter how close the created comes to the creator, there must remain an ontological gap between them, a distance that allows for the superiority of the creator because of its transcendence.

It is only through the denial of that ontological gap, through the rigorous commitment to the univocity of being, that an ontology of immanence can be created. "The significance of Spinozism seems to me to be this: it asserts immanence as a principle and frees expression from any subordination to emanative or exemplary causality.... And such a result can be obtained only within a perspective of univocity."[13]

The univocity of being threatens the Judeo-Christian conception of God by maintaining the equality of all being. For Deleuze, this is good news. If there is no longer a transcending God whose dictates we must follow or whose substance we must seek in our own lives to resemble, if there is no longer a transcending *Other* that can lay claim upon our faith or our behavior, then the door is open to an ontology of difference. Whatever our relation to the Spinozist God might be, it will not be articulated in terms of *following* or *subordinating* or *resembling*. These concepts imply an identity to which our actions, thoughts, and beliefs must return rather than a difference that can give them play, draw them farther afield of themselves.

But the univocity of being leads to its own philosophical puzzle. If all being is one, if there are no distinctions between levels or types or layers of being, then how are we to understand the distinctions between substance, attribute, and mode? If being is univocal, then what marks the difference between an attribute and the substance of which it is an attribute, the mode and the attribute it modifies?

---

[13] Deleuze, *Expressionism in Philosophy: Spinoza*, p. 180.

This puzzle threatens to undo the opening onto difference that the denial of transcendence was meant to offer us. If all being is univocal, if there are no distinctions to be drawn among types of being, if we deny not merely the hierarchy of substances but the internal distinctions among types of substance, then we seem to be left with a self-subsistent identity, one that does not give us difference but denies the very possibility of difference. Does the univocity of being lead us here?

What is required in order to solve this puzzle is a concept that allows for differences between and among attributes and modes without retreating to an ontology of transcendence. What is required is the concept of *expression*. Substance expresses itself in attributes, of which thought and extension are the only two accessible to human consciousness. Attributes, in turn, express themselves in the modes that are expressions or modifications of those attributes.

Deleuze writes,

Attributes are for Spinoza dynamic and active forms. And here at once we have what seems essential: attributes are no longer attributed, but they are in some sense "attributive." . . . As long as we conceive the attribute as something attributed, we thereby conceive a substance of the same species or genus; such a substance . . . is dependent on the goodwill of a transcendent God . . . On the other hand, as soon as we posit the attribute as "attributive" we conceive it as attributing its essence to something that remains identical for all attributes, that is, to necessarily existing substance.[14]

Attributes are "dynamic and active forms" that attribute their essences to substance. They are active expressions of substance. If substance (or, as Spinoza has it, "God, or substance") is expressive, it expresses itself in attributes, which are then not *things* that *emanate* from substance, but are instead substance expressing itself. "What do [attributes] attribute, what do they express? Each attribute attributes an infinite essence, that is, an unlimited quality."[15] Thought is an unlimited quality. Extension is an unlimited quality. For Spinoza, there are an infinite number of unlimited qualities, but humans can know only these two. Each unlimited quality is an essence of substance, which

---

[14] Deleuze, *Expressionism in Philosophy: Spinoza*, p. 45.
[15] Deleuze, *Expressionism in Philosophy: Spinoza*, p. 45.

is expressed through each attribute. Attributes attribute, or express, an essence. Substance expresses itself through its attributes.

This is not a static picture of substance standing behind a set of attributes that it has brought into existence. That would be a picture of attributes as created by or emanating from substance. That is the picture most of us would likely have in mind, since it is the one that has dominated the philosophical and religious tradition. For Deleuze, there are two differences between this picture of the relation of substance and attributes and Spinoza's. First, substance is woven into the attributes that express it. They are not separate from it. Being is univocal. Second, substance is not like a thing that gives birth to other things. It is more like a process of expression. Substance has a temporal character. It is bound up with time. To understand this temporal character of substance will require the introduction of Bergson's thought. But we must already remove ourselves from the temptation to see substance as an object or a thing if we are to grasp the Spinoza that Deleuze puts before us.

Attributes, in their turn, express themselves in modes. Deleuze often speaks of modes as particular things, and in this he is not wrong. However, this way of speaking may obscure the temporal character of those things. If we think of modes as modifications or even modulations of attributes, we are probably closer to the rhythm of Spinoza's thought. A modulation is not a product separate from its producer. It is a specific inflection of the producer. Every time a piece of music is played, it is a modulation of the composer's score.

If modes are modulations of attributes, then they are no more divorced from substance than those attributes are. Being remains univocal, although it is expressed first in attributes and then in modes. The difference between attributes and modes is that modes are conceivable only through the attributes they express, while attributes do not require any specific mode in order to be conceived. "*Attributes are thus forms common to God, whose essence they constitute, and to modes or creatures which imply them essentially*. . . . modes are only comprehended under these forms, while God, on the other hand, is convertible with them."[16] A man is an expression of thought and extension, and so an expression of those attributes and of substance. God, however, does

---

[16] Deleuze, *Expressionism in Philosophy: Spinoza*, p. 47.

not require man. Neither do the attributes of thought or extension. They could have expressed themselves in other ways, and often do.

Here is an analogy of expression. It is a bit simple, but may begin to capture the point. Japanese origami is the folding of paper into different recognizable figures: swans, turtles, people, trees. In origami, there is no cutting of the paper. No outside elements are introduced into it. Everything happens as an expression of that particular piece of paper. It is only the paper that is folded and unfolded into new arrangements, those arrangements being the modes of the paper, which is the origami's substance. The extension of the paper would be its attribute. If we can imagine the paper's being able to fold and unfold itself, we come closer to the concept of expression. Further, we must see each figure as part of a process, not a finished product, if we are to grasp the temporal character of substance.

Deleuze invokes the medieval concepts of explication, involvement, and complication in order to capture the concept of expression. "To explicate is to evolve, to involve is to implicate.... Expression is on the one hand an explication, an unfolding of what expresses itself, the One manifesting itself in the Many... Its multiple expression, on the other hand involves Unity. The One remains involved in what expresses it, imprinted in what unfolds it, immanent in whatever manifests it."[17]

Folding, unfolding, refolding. Like Japanese origami. It is a concept that Deleuze relies on twenty years later when he writes his book on Leibniz. But already, in the book on Spinoza, there is a complicity between Spinoza and Leibniz regarding the concept of expression. "To the extent that one may speak of the Anticartesianism of Leibniz and Spinoza, such Anticartesianism is grounded in the idea of expression."[18]

Folding, unfolding, refolding. Substance folds, unfolds, and refolds itself in its attributes and its modes, to which it remains immanent. It is always substance that, in folding and unfolding itself, remains within those folds. Being is univocal: there is no distinction between layers, levels, or types of being. There is no transcendence, only immanence.

The concept of complication completes the picture. It retains the unity of the one that unfolds itself. "Damascius develops the

[17] Deleuze, *Expressionism in Philosophy: Spinoza*, p. 16.
[18] Deleuze, *Expressionism in Philosophy: Spinoza*, p. 17.

description of this aspect of Being – in which the Multiple is collected, concentrated, *comprised* in the One, but in which the One also *explicates* itself in the Many – to great lengths. . . . All things are present to God, who complicates them. God is present to all things, which explicate and implicate him."[19] The One expresses itself in the Many, but does not become lost or dispersed in the Many. It is within them; they are within it. We may read Deleuze as saying nothing else in *Difference and Repetition* when he speaks in his own voice (not through Spinoza or any of the other figures that are the object of his earlier works): "Being is said in a single and same sense of everything of which it is said, but that of which it is said differs: it is said of difference itself."[20]

Spinoza's is the first fully developed thought of immanence. Three concepts are entwined to develop this thought: the univocity of being, immanence, and expression. This is what makes Spinoza the Christ of philosophers. No longer are we asked to submit ourselves to a transcendent being or Being who holds sway over what we are to become. No longer is resemblance or copying or obeying the proper mode of living for a human being. No longer is there a beyond whose superiority stands as a judgment against our world. There is only one being; it exists within all of the forms within which it manifests itself; those forms evolve and involve it while it, in turn, complicates them. This is the Good News he brings us.

IV

The question of how one might live, when Deleuze asks it, offers itself to two interpretations. One interpretation, the practical one, concerns the possibilities for living in which one might engage. The one who might engage in those ways of living is not always a human; it is not any "natural kind," as though the universe came with a set of instructions telling us how to divide it into specific kinds, as though there were not a multitude of ways of dividing, of individuating, the substance of the universe. The reason why Deleuze resists individuating into specifically

---

[19] Deleuze, *Expressionism in Philosophy: Spinoza*, p. 175.

[20] Deleuze, *Difference and Repetition*, p. 36. Although Deleuze distances himself slightly from Spinoza here: "Spinoza's substance appears independent of the modes, while the modes are dependent on substance, but as though on something other than themselves. Substance must be said *of* the modes and only *of* the modes." p. 40.

human beings (or anything else) as a natural category, why he resists what has come to be called "humanism," is beginning to emerge.

There is only one substance, and it can modify itself in many ways. Those ways are not copies or replicas or models of some original; they are foldings, unfoldings, refoldings of substance. Those foldings and unfoldings may become different from what they are. Darwin has taught us that they likely will. We do not even know of what a body is capable.

But there is a deeper issue. Deciding which things are the folds is a matter for judgment; the universe does not teach us this. There is only the ongoing process of substance. Whether it should be divided into humans or energy or libido or material relations is a question with no single answer because there is no single way to resolve it. To think in terms of univocity, immanence, and expression is to reject the division of being into natural kinds and to open up the horizon of a thought that embraces both its temporal fluidity and its resistance to rigid classification.

The second interpretation of the question of how one might live is ontological. It is a question of how living might go, what it might be to be alive. Deleuze's Spinoza has created concepts that import the vibrancy of life not only into organic beings but into the entirety of the universe. By abandoning transcendence in favor of immanence and by turning immanence into an expressive substance, Spinoza animates the universe. "To be is *to express oneself, to express something else, or to be expressed.*"[21] There is life everywhere, because everywhere there are foldings, unfoldings, and refoldings of the only substance there is. Indeed, substance is nothing other than those foldings, unfoldings, and refoldings. How might one live? How might it be that living goes? It might be that living invests the universe. It might be that the attempt to restrict the idea of living to functioning organic matter is too restrictive. Perhaps, instead of jettisoning ontology for something more empirical or more deconstructive, we might begin to construct and arrange concepts in a way that finds life everywhere.

But if life is everywhere, it is because expression is the way of the universe, because the substance of the universe is not so much a thing as a process. How does this process work? How does expression

[21] Deleuze, *Expressionism in Philosophy: Spinoza*, p. 253.

occur? According to what principles does immanence fold, unfold, and refold? Can ontology create concepts that can offer a glimpse of the character of being's expression?

These, ultimately, are questions about time. They are questions about the nature of time. They ask after the temporal character of expression. It is here that the son discovers the father.

V

If Spinoza is Deleuze's Christ of philosophers, then Bergson is the Father. Spinoza announces the Good News: immanence. But the Good News requires temporality in order to give it philosophical birth. The concept of immanence, if it is not to regress into a mindless sameness, must have recourse to another concept, that of expression. We have seen this. But expression is a temporal concept. Expression happens temporally; for Deleuze, expression is so inseparable from temporality that we might think of expression and temporality as the same thing, seen from two different angles. What Spinoza creates with his concept of expression and what Bergson creates with his concept of temporality are a seamless weave in Deleuze's philosophical perspective.

If this is so, then temporality as Bergson conceives it must be as foreign to our usual conception of time as Spinoza's concept of substance is to our usual conception of God. It is.

We are familiar with the standard view of time. It is a line, infinitely divisible and infinitely extended.

Time is divisible into epochs, years, months, days, hours, and seconds. Those seconds are divisible, and what those seconds are divisible into are themselves divisible. The division can proceed without end, instants within instants. The Now that we think of as the present instant is simply an ideal point. It can never be reached, because however thinly we slice the instant of the Now, we can always slice it thinner. In reality, there is no Now; that is simply a way of speaking.

Time is also infinitely extended. However far into the past we delve, we can always conceive an instant before that. There may have been nothing else before the stuff that was the source of the Big Bang; but there was time. There was the instant before the Big Bang, and the instant before the stuff that exploded came into existence, and the instant before that. The seconds, days, and epochs unfolded, even if there was nothing to unfold in them, nothing else but silence. And what goes for the past goes likewise for the future. However far into the future we project, we can always conceive an instant after that: the silence at the other end of time. Or better, since time has no end, the silence at the other end of what happens in time.

Bergson calls this conception of time a "spatialized" conception. It has the character of extension: a line that extends from one point infinitely remote to another point infinitely distant. The instants that occupy it, while ideal points, are each discrete from one another. They are like objects in space; however close they come to each other, they never overlap. There cannot be two objects, or two instants, in the same space and time. Time is also spatialized because it is conceived as a container. Things happen *in* time. Time is exterior to those things that happen; it marks them, each with its own moment, but is not absorbed by them. In fact, before anything happened (if there is such a before), there was time. After everything is done happening, there will still be time.

We might say that time is in this way transcendent to what happens.

This conception of time is not the only one. There are others. Among less technologically developed peoples, there is frequently a circular view of time; history repeats itself like the seasons or the years. For those engaged in modern life, however, the linear view is the most common conception of time. It is useful for us. It helps arrange our daily lives according to the variety of tasks that face us: I will spend an hour writing today and each day at the same time until this book is done, then I will move on to meet my other responsibilities. It co-ordinates action among people involved in disparate activities: at ten o'clock each of us will drop our specialized task and meet together in the conference room. It gives narrative form to lives that are often seen as individual rather than communal projects: first I was a medical student, then a resident . . .

Over the course of the twentieth century this conception of time has been challenged. First by the philosopher Edmund Husserl, then by Martin Heidegger and Jean-Paul Sartre, the linear, spatialized conception of time has been replaced by a more existential view of time. Time is not a container that exists outside the unfolding of a human life. Rather, it is something that is lived first and only afterwards given linear form. The latter is built upon the former, not the other way around.

In lived time there is not an equal weight according to each instant, as there is in the linear conception. The past, present, and future have distinct roles to play, of which the future is the dominant dimension. Human beings are characterized by our projects, by the direction in which we are headed, the plans that lie ahead of us. We look forward. It is the future, then, that carries the other dimensions of time along with it, like a comet carries its tail. This does not mean that the past has no bearing on how the future is lived. It does. The future is often seen by means of the orientation the past has given us. Our experiences do not simply drop away when they are over; rather, they accrete in us, they sediment into a thickness that orients us in some ways and not in others. Certain futures become open to us based on our past; others do not. Certain personal styles become ours; others do not. The past is swept up into the future, coloring and directing it. The future is where the past is taken up, where it has its effects.

There are those for whom the past carries more weight than the future can bear, those who cannot move beyond their past. For them the future is simply a continued confrontation with their past. This is the sign of psychological illness, a lived time that does not stop orienting itself toward the future but deforms that future in order to make it a repetition of the past. Failed projects are still engaged in, old wounds continue to bleed. Psychological illness is not, however, a privileging of the past. It is an orientation that, as for those without such illnesses, moves toward the future. The difference between illness and normality is that for the former that future is weighted with unrealized and often unrealizable projects that stem from past experience and that continue to press the urgency of their goals.

The present is where the future and past meet, the place of their mingling. The linear conception of time offers a certain privilege to the present. It is the only point of time that actually exists at a certain moment, even if its duration is too small to conceive. The present is the model for the proper unit of time. It is the (ideal) instant that is attached to those instants that are no longer and those that are not yet in order to form the line that is time. For the existential view of lived time, the present would be empty if it were not for the pull of the future and the weight of the past that give it its character. The present does not define the character of future and past. It is defined by them.

Neither the linear nor the existential conceptions of time are capable of giving birth to the ontological immanence Spinoza has offered us. The linear conception cannot capture the process of expression. In expression, the expressing substance remains within its expressions. It is not disconnected from them. It is not as though at one moment there is one thing and at another there is something else. The folds of substance are not something other than substance; they are substance itself, in the process of its folding (unfolding, refolding). The linear conception of time is blind to this, because it ignores the internal connection of the instants that compose it. It is more nearly akin to creationist or emanationist models, in which something emerges from something else. In spatializing time, in putting its instants beside one another rather than inside them, the linear conception of time is incapable of conceiving expression, and therefore loses all purchase on Spinoza's concept of immanence.

The existential conception of time does not do this. For Husserl, Heidegger, and Sartre, the dimensions of time, while distinct, do not exist at a remove from one another. The past is woven into the future; the future carries the past with it; the present is the moment where they are both realized. No dimension of time exists in the way that it does without incorporating the others. One can imagine expression finding a home in the existential conception of time. What begins in the past expresses itself in the future by means of the present; the future becomes an expression of the past, an expression that does not merely repeat it, but that unfolds it, or folds it, or refolds it.

The difficulty with the existential conception of time does not lie with the concept of expression. It lies elsewhere. The existential approach emphasizes the human character of time. It is subjectively oriented. What gives the future its privilege as a dimension of time is that we humans are characterized by our projects, by the goals and aspirations we place before ourselves. It is we who are defined by our futures. To define time in this way is to place it in service of human beings.

The existential conception of time denies the multiplicity of the "one" in the question of how one might live. It freezes the one into a humanistic model. This should not be surprising. Existentialism is a humanistic philosophy.[22] It is not so by mistake but by design. Deleuze's

[22] It is for this reason that Heidegger's later philosophy comes to reject the existential elements of the earlier works.

philosophy is not humanistic. It does not seek to create an ontology centered on human perceptions or the human orientation toward the world. This does not mean that humans do not figure in his ontology. Nor does it mean that we, as humans, do not figure in his approach to temporality. What it means is that we cannot occupy pride of place in that approach. We must conceive temporality in a way that both captures the human living of time and does not subordinate all of temporality to it. "It is only to the extent that movement is grasped as belonging to things as much as to consciousness that it ceases to be confused with psychological duration, whose point of application it will displace, thereby necessitating that things participate directly in duration itself."[23]

It is Henri Bergson who provides the approach Deleuze requires. For Bergson, the human dimension of time opens out onto a wider horizon, one that neither denies nor privileges the human dimension. Further, this conception of time extends the concept of immanence; it offers a way to understand how expression occurs. If expression is temporal above all rather than spatial, then temporality itself must be conceived temporally rather than spatially. The concept of *duration* (*durée*) allows us to do that.

VI

Begin with psychological memory. I recall something that happened to me. My lover breaks up with me one night in a college town far from mine in the early autumn of my first year away from home. My grandmother and step-grandmother, after years of hatred, pose together for a picture at my mother's third wedding. I am dog-sledding in the Arctic. The ice is smooth and padded with a thin layer of snow. There are no sounds but those of the dogs kicking up a mist of flakes as they run. And I think to myself, for the first time in many years, life is good.

These are memories. They are recollections of things that have happened. They are not happening now but have happened in the past. Here is how the linear conception of time sees the past in which these things took place. It does not exist. It is no longer. Or better, it exists not in reality but only *as a memory* in the present, if indeed it is remembered. There is no past. There is only a series of presents that

[23] Deleuze, *Bergsonism*, p. 48.

become past, each yielding to another present. But how does each present move into past? What is the connection between that which is and that which no longer is? The present is a something that exists; the past is a nothing. How is it that this something becomes a nothing? How does the present pass?

The past and the present do not denote two successive moments, but two elements which coexist: One is the present, which does not cease to pass, and the other is the past, which does not cease to be but through which all presents pass.... The past does not follow the present, but on the contrary, is presupposed by it as the pure condition without which it would not pass.[24]

The present passes. With this recognition, we are already beyond the ken of the linear conception of time. For the linear conception, there is only Now, and Now is only an ideal point. It can have no real thickness because it is infinitely divisible; each instant can be divided into other instants. However small one carves the instants of time, one can always imagine them more finely carved. And what does it mean to carve these instants? It means that what is sliced off is separated from what is left, that the infinitely vanishing instant of time is separated from the past by the past's being "no longer," not really there any more. There is only an ideal point surrounded by the nothing of the past and the nothing of the future. The present does not pass. It cannot pass, because there is a gulf between the ideal point that is Now and the rest that is no longer. Husserl recognizes this point. He writes that in order for there to be a present that is lived, it must contain a "retention" of the immediate past and a "protention" of the immediate future, or else it would disappear into the nothing of its ideal point.[25] The "living present" has a thickness that extends backward into the immediate past and forward into the immediate future.

The present passes. In order for this to happen, there must *be* a past for the present to pass into. The past must exist as surely as does the present. It does not exist in the same way as the present. Bergson conceives it as existing in a very different way; it is a virtuality, in contrast to the actuality of the present. (The difference between a virtuality and an actuality will be discussed shortly.) But it must exist. Otherwise, the

[24] Deleuze, *Bergsonism*, p. 59.
[25] Husserl, *The Phenomenology of Internal Time-Consciousness.*

present could not pass. It would just disappear. And even that would be difficult to conceive, since what would disappear is infinitely small. Instead, we say that the present passes into the past, which exists and which is the pure condition of the present's ability to pass.

We are still in the realm of psychology. Husserl's existential conception of time serves as a corrective to the linear conception, but it is a corrective that relies on the lived time of a human consciousness. Bergson, in contrast, does not believe that memory is only psychological. It is ontological. There is psychological memory, to be sure. But psychological memory points to something larger than itself, to a wider ontological condition that contains it. For psychological memory, the past takes place in the present, in retention and in memory. That present, the living present, has a thickness that the linear conception of time cannot recognize. But it is a present nonetheless.

Ontological memory is concerned with the past itself, not simply with its existence in the present. "Strictly speaking, the psychological is the present. Only the present is 'psychological'; but the past is pure ontology; pure recollection has only ontological significance."[26]

Husserl's concept of retention (as well as his concept of recollection, the act of remembering) is psychological. It belongs to the "living present" of the existential conception of time. Bergson's concept of the past is not psychological; it is the ontological source from which psychological memory springs.

The past is not merely a psychological residue in the present. If it were, there would be many pasts, as many as there are people, or perhaps as many as there are psychological states of people. For Bergson there is one past, a single past in which all psychological memory participates. To understand this past is to understand how expression occurs, and to begin to understand the concept of difference that Nietzsche asks us to affirm.

The past does not exist in the same way as the present does. The present exists in *actuality*. We experience it directly. As the existentialists would say, we have phenomenological access to it. The past (not the psychological past of individuals but the ontological past) exists *virtually*. The virtual past is there; it is not nothing. It is not the past of

[26] Deleuze, *Bergsonism*, p. 56.

the linear conception of time. It is not an instant, or a thing. But it is there, in a different way from the way the present is there.

Think of genetic information. Our genes store information about us. They contribute that information in the process of our growth. But the information itself is not in the genes in any actual way. One cannot look at someone's genes under a microscope and find it lying there on the slide, available to vision. As the genes unfold, the information becomes apparent in the actual world; the person becomes what the information formatted that person to become. But the information itself, even though it exists, does not exist in actuality. It exists virtually in the structure of the genes.[27]

We may think of virtuality that way, as something that exists but not in actuality. As Deleuze says, the virtual actualizes itself (the genetic information unfolds as a person), but it is not actual.

Deleuze often cautions against a mistake that can be made in thinking about the virtual. The distinction between the virtual and the actual is not the same as the distinction between the possible and the real. There are two differences. First, the possible does not exist, while the virtual does. It is real. *"The virtual is real in so far as it is virtual."*[28] The possible is what might become or might have become real, but as yet has not. The virtual is already real. It does not need to have anything added to it in order to become real.

The second difference is that the possible is a mirror of the real, while the virtual does not mirror the actual. The possible is structured like the real, missing only its characteristic of really existing. The possibility of my finishing the writing of this chapter today is exactly like my finishing it today, except that it will not happen in reality. The possible is an image of the real, constructed just like it minus the real's character of factual existence. Or, seen from the other direction, the real is the image of the possible, with the addition that it is a real image.

The absence of reality does not mean that the possible is inferior to the real. It may be that the possible is superior, and that the real fails to reach the standards it sets. The possibility of my finishing writing this

---

[27] There is more to say about genes and virtuality, since the situation is more complex than this paragraph indicates. The next chapter discusses genes in more detail.

[28] Deleuze, *Difference and Repetition*, p. 208.

chapter today is not inferior to my really not finishing it. But whether superior, inferior, or neither, the possible and the real mirror each other.

The virtual is not an image of the actual, or of anything else. It is not like an image. It is not the actual minus the characteristic of actuality. The past is not like the present. It is structured differently. Think of the relation of substance to attributes and modes. Attributes and modes unfold (fold, refold) substance, but not as copies for which substance provides the original model. Although substance actualizes itself in attributes and modes, its way of being as virtual is not simply a mirror image of its way of being as actual modes.

Deleuze uses the distinction between the terms virtual/actual and possible/real in order to distance himself from Platonic ways of thinking. For Plato, Forms are the original, existing things the copies. Existing things are truer realizations of forms the more they participate in them, that is, the closer they come to resembling those Forms. The ideas of model and copy and of resemblance carry transcendence in their train. The model is the superior transcendent, the copy the inferior existent. The copy takes its value only by resemblance to the model. This is a denigration of existing things, the second characteristic of transcendence. Deleuze rejects the denigration of existence, and with it both the distinctions between model and copy on the one hand and possible and real on the other. Both distinctions, by relying on the concept of resemblance, compare what is in existence to something outside by means of which the existence is judged.

The virtual is neither a ghost of the actual nor a transcendent that hovers above it. It is part of the real, just as actuality is. No more and no less. But it is not real in the same way as the actual. How does this distinction help us to understand the ontological past and its relation to the present? To say that the present actualizes the past is true, but not very informative. What is the past like? What is the present like? How do the two relate?

Bergson uses the image of an inverted cone to describe the past. The summit of the cone intersects with the plane that is the present. "If I represent by a cone SAB, the totality of the recollections accumulated in my memory, the base AB, situated in the past, remains motionless, while the summit S, which indicates at all times my present, moves forward unceasingly, and unceasingly also touches the moving plane

P of my actual representation of the universe."[29] The imagery here is of psychological memory: *my* memory, *my* actual representation. For Deleuze, however, Bergson is already on the ground of the ontological past. It is not merely *my* past that exists like a cone in relation to my present; it is *the* past. My past is a particular perspective on the ontological past in which it participates.

Why the image of a cone? A cone is three-dimensional. Its base extends away from its summit in a widening sweep. What do these aspects of a cone have to do with the ontological past? There are different layers of the past, and these layers exist as different degrees of "contraction" or "expansion."

The past AB coexists with the present S, but by including in itself all the sections A'B', A"B", etc., that measure the degrees of a purely ideal proximity or distance in relation to S. Each of these sections is *virtual*, belonging to the being in itself of the past. Each of these sections or each of these levels includes not particular elements of the past, but always the totality of the past. It includes this totality at a more or less expanded or contracted level.[30]

What is contraction and expansion (or relaxation, as Deleuze some-times puts it)? It cannot be a matter of being further past, further from the present. The more remote past is not more expanded than the re-cent past, even though the greatest degree of contraction does occur with the present. "The totality of the past" exists at each section or level. There is only one time, the time that includes both the present and the past, always together, always "at the same time." It is this that Bergson is after in constructing the concept of duration.

For Bergson, a greater contraction means a closer relation to a person's behavioral involvement with the world. "We tend to scatter ourselves over AB in the measure that we detach ourselves from our sensory and motor state to live in the life of dreams; we tend to con-centrate ourselves in S in the measure that we attach ourselves more firmly to the present reality, responding by motor reactions to sensory stimulation."[31] Deleuze offers an example of contraction in discussing sensory perception: "What, in fact, is a sensation? It is the operation of

---

[29] Bergson, *Matter and Memory*, p. 152.
[30] Deleuze, *Bergonism*, p. 60.
[31] Bergson, *Matter and Memory*, pp. 162–3.

contracting trillions of vibrations onto a receptive surface."[32] A more contracted past is one in which the elements of the entire past are brought closer to a particular person's engagement with the world.

But it is always the whole of the past that is contracted, not simply the more recent past. Marcel Proust begins to capture this idea in a passage from *Remembrance of Things Past*:

> ... the differences which exist between every one of our real impressions – differences which explain why a uniform depiction of life cannot bear much resemblance to the reality – derive probably from the following cause: the slightest word that we have said, the most insignificant action that we have performed at any one epoch of our life was surrounded by, and colored by the reflection of, things which logically had no connection with it and which later have been separated from it by our intellect which could make nothing of it for its own rational purposes, things, however, in the midst of which – here the pink reflection of the evening upon the flower-covered wall of a country restaurant, a feeling of hunger, the desire for women, the pleasure of luxury; there the blue volutes of the morning sea and, enveloped in them, phrases of music half emerging like the shoulders of water-nymphs – the simplest act or gesture remains immured as within a thousand vessels, each one of them filled with things of a color, a scent, a temperature that are absolutely different one from another, vessels, moreover, which being disposed over the whole range of our years, during which we have never ceased to change if only in our dreams and our thoughts, are situated at the most various moral altitudes and give us the sensation of extraordinarily diverse atmospheres.[33]

And there is more. It is not just the entirety of *my* past that exists within me; it is the entirety of the past *itself*. My own past, my sensations, desires, memories, joys, do not arise outside the historical context in which I live. They arise within a legacy that is planted in me by history, a legacy that I might perhaps change but cannot escape. To live is to navigate the world immersed in a historically given context that is not of one's own making. Thus my own past is a participant in, and at the same time a perspective on, the past itself. That past exists within me, and appears at each moment I am engaged with the world.

---

[32] Deleuze, *Bergsonism*, p. 74.

[33] Proust, *Remembrance of Things Past: The Past Recaptured*, p. 132. Compare this passage with one from Deleuze in his book on Proust: "Perhaps that is what time is: the ultimate existence of parts, of different sizes and shapes, which cannot be adapted, which do not develop at the same rhythm, and which the stream of style does not sweep along at the same speed." *Proust and Signs*, p. 101.

It is in this engagement that the actualization of the virtual occurs. A person, through action or memory or perception, brings the past to bear upon the present moment. An action may bring previous learning to bear in the discovery of a solution to a puzzle; a memory may recall, within the present context, a past moment that one is reminded of; a perception sees what is in front of one within the horizon of the past that one has lived through and the legacy of one's history. In all these cases, the past and present are mingled: the past unfolding, the present creating and inventing.

Always, three things must be borne in mind. *There is no present that does not actualize the past. It is all of the past that is actualized at every moment. The past that is actualized exists.* The actualization of the past by a person is the psychological moment. The virtual past that is actualized is the ontological moment. "In this way a psychological unconscious, distinct from the ontological unconscious, is defined. The latter corresponds to a recollection that is pure, virtual, impassive, inactive, *in itself.* The former represents the movement of recollection in the course of actualizing itself."[34]

But the psychological moment and the ontological moment, while distinct, are inseparable. Actualization is not only psychological; it is also ontological. And the virtual is coiled in every human psyche. The past is not a monolith, a block. It is lived in actualization, just as actualization emerges from the field of the virtual.

The temporal character of Spinoza's substance is beginning to come into view. Substance is duration, the virtual that is always there in all of its modes. Actualization is the "modalizing" of the virtual, the folding, unfolding, and refolding of the virtual into modes. This actualization, this "modalization," is not a making of one thing into another. It is not a creation or an emanation. It is a process in which substance expresses itself in the course of its folding, unfolding, and refolding.

Is Spinoza's substance the same as Bergson's ontological past, the same as duration? If the issue is one of historical accuracy, of fidelity to precise philosophical positions, the answer is, no. Deleuze himself resists making the comparison, and for good reasons. Each philosopher has created his own concepts to solve his own problems. The problem of God for Spinoza is not the same problem as that of time for Bergson. Moreover, it is not an issue of historical accuracy. It is a question of

[34] Deleuze, *Bergsonism*, p. 71.

constructing concepts, using what Spinoza and Bergson have given us in order to create an ontology that can address the question of how one might live. Deleuze sees that Spinoza's immanence and Bergson's duration can be brought together in constructing a philosophy that allows us to see living more vitally than we had before. That is what Deleuze seeks.[35]

If the past, if duration, is always there virtually, and if it actualizes itself in the present, then what is the past? What is its nature and character? It is not simply what has happened. That would be the past seen through the lens of the linear conception of time; the past as what has gone before, the past as what is no longer. Proust gives us an indication of the nature of the past in the passage above. The impressions of our past are "surrounded" and "colored by . . . things which logically had no connection with it." Our gestures and acts are "immured" in vessels in which the surrounding elements "are absolutely different one from another." What characterizes duration is not logical connection; nor is it relation among similar elements, nor is it identification or imitation or resemblance. It is difference that characterizes duration: "Duration *is that which differs with itself.*"[36]

The past, duration, is characterized by a certain kind of difference, a kind of difference that cannot be subsumed under the categories of identity. Here is a difference that would be subsumed under categories of identity. An ironing board and a shoe are different. They are different because there is such a thing as an ironing board (an identity) and a shoe (another identity), and those identities are not identical with each other. They are different. Here difference means something like "not identical."

For some philosophers, for example G. W. F. Hegel, difference appears in the form of opposition. This is difference as seen through the dialectic. A perception that appears immediately to me, without being brought into linguistic categories, is opposed to linguistically mediated perception ("It's a chair" or "It's red"). The immediate and mediated

---

35 In *Dialogues*, he writes, "The history of philosophy has always been the agent of power in philosophy, and even in thought. It has played the represser's role: how can you think without having read Plato, Descartes, Kant and Heidegger, and so-and-so's book about them? A formidable school of intimidation which manufactures specialists in thought – but which also makes those who stay outside conform all the more to this specialism which they despise." p. 13.

36 Deleuze, "La conception de la différence chez Bergson," p. 88 (my translation).

are opposites. Hegel sometimes says that each is the negation of the other. In the course of the dialectic, these oppositions will need to be mediated into a higher unity that will eliminate their opposition. The immediate character of perception and its linguistic mediation will need to be reconciled, their opposition overcome.[37] This is a more sophisticated form of difference, but one that is still subsumed under categories of identity. The identity of the immediate is opposed to the identity of the mediated, although in the end they will both be subsumed. But they will be subsumed into a higher identity that captures them both. Difference here is still in thrall to identity.

The difference that Proust discusses is not a difference between identities. The gestures and acts he refers to do not retain their character as identical to themselves when they become part of the past. They dissolve and reform in different ways. There is no gesture, no act, that can retain its particular character, that can, so to speak, be what it is. A particular gesture loses its specific character when it changes surroundings or comes in contact with other parts of the past. The past then is not composed of elements that are identical to themselves, and thus the past itself has no particular identity. One way to put that point would be to say that it *differs with itself.*

Deleuze does not believe that all difference is like this. There are differences between identities: the ironing board is different from the shoe. There are oppositions and negations of the kind Hegel discusses. Those differences do exist; but they don't exist in duration. They exist in the present. They are spatial rather than temporal differences. Deleuze sometimes uses the term "multiplicity" for difference. He writes that there are

two types of multiplicity. One is represented by space . . . It is a multiplicity of exteriority, of simultaneity, of juxtaposition, of order, of quantitative differentiation, of *difference in degree*; it is a numerical multiplicity, *discontinuous and actual.* The other type of multiplicity appears in pure duration: It is an internal multiplicity of succession, of fusion, of organization, of heterogeneity, of qualitative discrimination, or of *difference in kind*; it is a *virtual and continuous* multiplicity that cannot be reduced to numbers."[38]

---

[37] This overcoming is a long and complex story in Hegel's thought, and the reconciliation a subtle one. Deleuze does not want to deny this, but rather to critique the terms in which that story is told.

[38] Deleuze, *Bergsonism*, p. 38.

The problem is that "People have seen only differences in degree where there are differences in kind."[39]

Duration is a virtual multiplicity, a realm of difference where differences are not between previously constituted identities but where difference "differs with itself." This virtual multiplicity, this realm of temporal difference is as real as the realm of spatial identities and differences that everyday experience presents us with. It is from the realm of duration that the present arises, as its virtuality actualizes into specific spatial features. Thus, "the Bergsonian revolution is clear: We do not move from the present to the past, from perception to recollection, but from the past to the present, from recollection to perception."[40]

What is more, duration does not only give rise to the present; it is also of the present. Spinoza's lesson must not be lost. Immanence requires that the virtuality of duration not only actualize itself in the present, but that it is of the very present that it actualizes. The present – the realm of space, identities, and differences between those identities (differences in degree) – does not emanate or separate itself from the past of duration.

VII

The immanence of duration to the present has an important consequence: the present always has a greater potential for transformation than it appears to have. Why is this? The present "presents" itself to us as the realm of identities and differences in degrees. In the spatial present, things appear to have more or less fixed identities. An ironing board is nothing more than an ironing board, a shoe nothing more than a shoe. But if difference is immanent to the present, then each moment is suffused by a realm of difference that lies coiled within it, offering the possibility of disrupting any given identity. There is always more than presents itself, a surplus beyond what is directly experienced. That surplus is not another fixed identity, a "something else," but the virtuality of difference with no identity and all measure of potential.

---

[39] Deleuze, *Bergsonism*, p. 23.
[40] Deleuze, *Bergsonism*, p. 63.

This is easier to conceive if we think temporally than if we think spatially, which is why Bergson is so important for Deleuze. Thinking spatially, we ask ourselves: How can an ironing board be anything more than an ironing board? The idea that there is anything more around it or inside it seems absurd. It would be like positing a mystical horizon or aura around or within physical objects that somehow lets them be more than they are.[41] But if we think temporally the idea of a virtual difference makes more sense. The present is more than simply an ideal Now, cut off from past and future. Rather, it is a realm of spatial presence, of relatively fixed identities and of differences in degree, suffused by a past that both contributes to those identities and helps to undercut them, to unsettle them in ways that allow for expressions other than the ones that appear at a given moment in experience.

Here we discover the wisdom of Spinoza's use of the concept of substance. If Deleuze is right in saying that Spinoza sometimes leans too heavily toward the idea that substance is independent of its modes, we must recognize on the other hand that substance is not simply reducible to its modes. There is always more to the modes than the modes themselves; there is the substance that is immanent to them.

And there is always more to the present than the present reveals to us. There is the realm of virtual difference that is immanent to it. The world both is and is not as it seems. If we think spatially, the world is as it seems, exhausted by its identities and distinguished by differences of degree. If we think temporally with Bergson, the world is always more than it seems, always fraught with differences that can actualize themselves in novel and unfamiliar ways.

Ontology is beginning to reveal itself as more than an inventory for what philosophers have said exists. It has more to offer than a pallid reinforcement of what presents itself to us as natural or inevitable. Ontology is not merely a sop for conformism. This is because, for Deleuze, ontology is not a study of what is, if by that we mean a study of the identities of things. It is a study of what is and of what unsettles it. It is a study that creates concepts that may open out onto new lands, onto terrains that have yet to be traveled. Nomadism, the wandering among

---

[41] Actually, it is not quite so absurd as that, even from the standpoint of science. I have tried to capture this point in Deleuze's treatment of science in my "Deleuze, Science, and Difference."

those lands, plays a significant role in Deleuze's later thought. Its seeds lie here. Foucault and Derrida are right to say that most ontologies lead to conformism, to a blind confirmation of what we are told is already there. But this is not because it is the fate of ontology to do so. It is because ontology has been dominated, throughout the course of its long history, by transcendence and spatiality. In reading Spinoza and Bergson together, Deleuze appropriates and creates concepts that challenge this domination. It is not transcendence and spatiality that are the proper terms for ontological thinking; it is immanence and temporality. Immanence and temporality remove ontology, and philosophy generally, from the sad, withered task of ratifying a status quo, which has no need of philosophy in the first place, to the creation of concepts that see the status quo as only one ontological arrangement among many.

We do not even know of what a body is capable.

VIII

The coiling of difference within seemingly fixed identities is the consequence of the immanence of duration to the present. The past does not trail the present, but is intimate with it. We do not move from present to past but from past to present.

But what about the future? What is the role of the future in the temporally oriented ontology that Deleuze is constructing? We have seen the intimate relationship of past to present, present to past. Is there no future here? And if there is, how are we to conceive it?

This question cannot be answered without recourse to the third member of the Trinity: the Holy Ghost, Nietzsche.

IX

The Nietzschean spirit haunts much of twentieth-century philosophy, particularly, but not solely, in the Continental tradition. Nietzsche is at once angel and demon. He is the philosopher far ahead of his time, pointing the way toward philosophy's future; he is the threat of nihilism and relativism that any true philosophy must avoid. He is the standard bearer for much of post–World War II French philosophy; he is the evidence that that philosophy is bankrupt. There is no philosophy that does not operate in his shadow, whether to cloak itself in his darkness or to escape it into the light.

Deleuze is no exception. He can be read as a straightforward disciple of Nietzsche. His concepts can be interpreted as extensions of Nietzsche's, from immanence to difference to nomadism. Deleuze's anti-conformism sometimes seems, even to Deleuze, to be of a piece with Nietzsche's. "Marx and Freud," Deleuze writes, "perhaps, do represent the dawn of our culture, but Nietzsche is something entirely different: the dawn of counterculture."[42]

To reduce Deleuze's thought to Nietzsche's would be too quick. Nietzsche can be interpreted in many ways. Taken in a certain way, he becomes a niche in which Deleuze's thought can be inserted. Taken in another way, the two seem more distant. If Nietzsche has resources that open new vistas for Deleuze, it is equally true that Deleuze's use of Nietzschean concepts can make Nietzsche seem fresh reading. What is most interesting about Nietzsche's influence on Deleuze is not the question of whether Deleuze's thought should be seen as distinct from Nietzsche's, or whether Deleuze's concepts are simply reinscriptions, but the way the spirit of Nietzsche suffuses his work. Nietzsche is Deleuze's Holy Ghost. The two are brothers in spirit, even where they are not philosophers of the same concepts. They are fellow travelers, fellow nomads, even where Deleuze's own interpretation – or appropriation – of a Nietzschean concept inverts the interpretation we have come to associate with it.

As is the case with the eternal return.

The eternal return has always been one of the most puzzling of Nietzschean concepts. Philosophers find it to be among the most obscure to understand. This is not because its meaning is difficult, or so it has seemed, but because its role in Nietzsche's overall philosophy is elusive. As far as its meaning goes, the eternal return is taken to be the cycling back of the same things over the course of time. In *Thus Spoke Zarathustra*, Zarathustra's animals taunt him with this. "Behold, we know what you teach: that all things recur eternally, and we ourselves too; and that we have already existed an eternal number of times, and all things with us. . . . I come again, with this sun, with this earth, with this eagle, with this serpent – *not* to a new life or a better life or a similar

[42] Deleuze, "Nomad Thought," p. 142.

life: I come back eternally to this same, selfsame life . . ."[43] It is a wound to Zarathustra to know that everything, even the smallest and pettiest of human foibles, will recur eternally. Nothing, not even the most resentful or most petty of people, will drop out of the cycle of return.

For Deleuze, the eternal return is not as it might seem. It is not the eternal return of the same: "According to Nietzsche the eternal return is in no sense a thought of the identical but rather a thought of synthesis, a thought of the absolutely different . . . It is not the 'same' or the 'one' which comes back in the eternal return but return is itself the one which ought to belong to diversity and to that which differs."[44] The eternal return is not the recurrence of the same; it is the recurrence of difference, of difference itself. The future will reveal itself to be the eternal return; and in the return will be found the affirmation of difference that is Deleuze's Nietzschean spirit.

Deleuze's definition of the eternal return is obscure. "*Return is the being of that which becomes.* Return is the being of becoming itself, the being which is affirmed in becoming."[45]

In traditional philosophy, being is contrasted with becoming. Being is that which endures, that which underlies, that which remains constant. Being is the source and the foundation, fixed and unchanging. God is being; Nature is being; for those philosophers who resist a Spinozist view, substance is being. On the other hand, becoming is ephemeral, changing, inconstant, and therefore less substantial than being. Being is real, becoming is a passing illusion.

What if things were the opposite of what they seem? What if there were no enduring being, only becoming? What if the only thing that is real is becoming, the changing and fluid character of that which is? Nietzsche believes this to be the case. "If the world had a goal, it must have been reached. If there were for it some unintended final state, this also must have been reached. If it were capable of pausing and becoming fixed, of 'being,' if in the whole course of its becoming it possessed even for a moment this capability of 'being,' then all becoming would long since have come to an end . . ."[46]

43 Nietzsche, *Thus Spoke Zarathustra*, pp. 332–3.
44 Deleuze, *Nietzsche and Philosophy*, p. 46.
45 Deleuze, *Nietzsche and Philosophy*, p. 24.
46 Nietzsche, *The Will to Power*, p. 546.

Deleuze concurs. "For there is no being beyond becoming, nothing beyond multiplicity; neither multiplicity nor becoming are appearances or illusions.... Multiplicity is the inseparable manifestation, essential transformation and constant symptom of unity. Multiplicity is the affirmation of unity; becoming is the affirmation of being."[47]

We are already prepared for this thought. The way has been paved by Spinoza and Bergson. Substance does not stand behind or outside its modes; if the modes change and evolve, that is because substance itself is folding, unfolding, and refolding. Substance is not a constant identity that stands behind the modes. Substance is becoming. Duration is not identity. It is difference, difference that may actualize itself into specific identities, but that remains difference even within those identities. There is no being here, at least not in the traditional sense. Or, to put the point another way, if there is being, if there is a constant, it is becoming itself: the folding and unfolding of substance, the actualization of duration. If we have a taste for paradox, which Deleuze does, we might say that the only being is the being of becoming.

And that being is multiplicity, difference. It is not a multiplicity that is a Many as opposed to a One. The One – duration, substance – is multiplicity itself. Multiplicity, difference, is not transcendent; it is immanent. Multiplicity is the affirmation of unity.

And return is the being of becoming. There is only becoming, and that becoming is the eternal return. What returns then? What is it that recurs eternally, always coming back to face us, never left behind? If the past actualizes itself in the present, if we move from past to present rather than from present to past, and if the past that actualizes itself in the present is difference, then *what recurs eternally is difference itself.* What faces us always is difference, difference in kind, difference that has yet to be congealed into identities.

Deleuze's reasoning here is rigorous, if difficult. With Spinoza, he says that all being is immanent, that there is no transcendence. There is no constant identity outside our world – no God, no laws of history, no goal – that dictates its character. This does not mean that nothing exists outside our experience. What is not outside our world may still be outside our experience. (Science has long taught us this.) But,

---

[47] Deleuze, *Nietzsche and Philosophy*, pp. 23–4.

whether it is within or outside our experience, there is no being that is not of our world.

With Bergson, Deleuze shows that substance is temporal in character, that it is a folding and unfolding in time in which that which folds, unfolds, and refolds is a past that is never gone. Moreover, that past is difference itself. There are no stable identities, only levels of contracted differences that may actualize themselves in the present.

What is the future, then? What is it that lies before us? Unactualized difference. We have already learned that if the past did not exist, the present itself could not pass. Now we are told that "The passing moment could never pass if it were not already past and yet to come – at the same time as being present."[48] Duration is a unity, but it is not merely a unity of past and present, as it might have seemed with Bergson. It is a unity of past, present, and future. As a unity, each dimension is woven into the others. The future, the present, the past are involved, each in the others.

The future has the character of the past. Just as the past is difference in kind, pure multiplicity, so is the future. It comes to meet us without any pregiven identities, any persevering constants. This does not mean that the future is empty; it means that the future is the return of virtual difference that characterizes the past as Bergson conceives it. What returns are not the identities that are actualized in the present. What returns is the virtuality that lies behind and within those identities.

It is not being that returns but rather the returning itself that constitutes being insofar as it is affirmed of becoming and of that which passes. It is not some one thing which returns but rather returning itself is the one thing which is affirmed of diversity or multiplicity. In other words, identity in the return does not describe the nature of that which returns but, on the contrary, the fact of returning for that which differs.[49]

The future is not empty; indeed, it is full to overflowing.

To say that the future has the character of past, then, is not to recall the tired cliché that history repeats itself. If that were the lesson

---

[48] Deleuze, *Nietzsche and Philosophy*, p. 48.
[49] Deleuze, *Nietzsche and Philosophy*, p. 48.

of the eternal return, it would have nothing to teach us. Everything returns, yes; everything recurs. But what recurs does not do so in the form of actualized identities but in the form of the virtual difference that constitutes those identities. The sun, the earth, the eagle and the serpent return. Even the smallest and meanest of emotions returns. But they do not return as the sun, the earth, the eagle, the serpent, the smallest and meanest of emotions. They return as the virtuality that constitutes them. The eternal return is the being of becoming, and the being of becoming is virtual difference, multiplicity.

The past is duration; the present is actualization; the future is eternal return. But within all these, constitutive of them, is difference. Difference in kind constitutes duration. Actualized difference constitutes the present. The return of difference constitutes the future.[50]

To affirm the eternal return, to embrace it, is the hardest task for Zarathustra. For to affirm it is not to say yes to the things of this world, to will them to return just as they are, each in its place. Rather, it is to affirm difference itself. It is to live by embracing a future that is not characterized by the continuity of the present, nor by the repetition of its actualizations, but by a difference that can never be brought fully into one's grasp. The future is outside one's control, conceptually and behaviorally. There is too much there: nothing that has to be there, so many things that can be.

Deleuze discusses the dice throw in the third part of Nietzsche's *Thus Spoke Zarathustra*. He says, "The game has two moments which are those of a dicethrow – the dice that is thrown and the dice that falls back. . . . The dice which are thrown once are the affirmation of *chance*, the combination which they form on falling is the affirmation of *necessity*."[51] What does this mean?

We face the future, which is the eternal return, the return of difference. There is nothing specific that has to be there in the future, but so much that can be. The future is virtual difference that has not yet actualized itself into a particular present. "Anything might happen," not simply in the pedestrian sense that we cannot predict the future,

---

[50] Constantin Boundas details this idea, particularly with regard to the future, in "Deleuze-Bergson: An Ontology of the Virtual."

[51] Deleuze, *Nietzsche and Philosophy*, p. 25–6.

but also and more deeply in the sense that the future itself is pure multiplicity. That is the throw of the dice. It is chance.[52]

Then the future actualizes itself in a present, as the past does. The return crystallizes into identities. Pure temporality becomes also spatiality. We are faced with a particular situation that has emerged from the multiplicity that has returned.

That is the combination, the dice that falls back. It is necessity. It is necessity not because things had to happen that way. Things might not have happened that way. There is no transcendence guiding the present, giving form to a particular future that has to happen this way and not others. The idea that this particular future and no other is going to become the present is just the kind of thinking Deleuze rejects. It has three faults. First, it implies that the future is constituted by particular identities, instead of being a virtual multiplicity of the kind Bergson conceives. Second, it implies that that future exists as a possibility before it becomes a reality, whereas Deleuze contrasts possibility with virtuality. Third, it implies guidance, which seems to require transcendence rather than immanence. In immanence, there is folding, unfolding, refolding. But there is no guiding force, no invisible hand.

The term *necessity* indicates that how the future is actualized is largely out of the control of any particular person or group of people. Nevertheless, it appears; it is inscribed in reality. It must be lived. To be sure, people can affect the future; we are not passive recipients of our lives. But we do not determine their shape. We are involved in a temporality that outstrips us, and that may constitute a present that we had not dreamed of but cannot escape.

I study medicine and become a doctor in order to develop a cure for cancer. Someone else discovers it before I do. Perhaps I was even on the wrong path, not because I was sloppy but because all the clues led me there. I will not discover the cure for cancer. That is how things unfolded. It might not have turned out that way. The person who discovered the cure might have been hit by a car, or been on the wrong path just as I was, or have misread some laboratory results. But none of these things happened, and the multiplicity of the future has now coalesced into a particular present.

---

[52] If the analogy were to be more rigorous, we would have to imagine the dice without any particular numbers yet etched onto their faces.

In 1987 the Palestinians start an uprising against the occupation of their land by Israel; in 1990 the Berlin Wall comes down; in 1991 the United States declares war on Iraq. These events change the nature of the Palestinian struggle for freedom. They become part of the necessity of being Palestinian. Does the Berlin Wall have to come down at that time? Does the United States have to declare war then, or at all? Are these events etched in the Laws of History? No. Before they happen, they do not need to happen; nothing makes them happen. But their occurrence makes them a necessity, a reality that could not be controlled but cannot now be avoided.

The dice are thrown. This is the eternal return. The dice are always thrown, at every moment, at every instant. The future is always with us, here and now, just as the past is. A pair of dice, loaded with the multiplicity that is duration, is thrown. The dice fall back. They show a combination. There you have it. Those are the numbers. That is your throw. You may get another, but it will not erase the combination that faces you. That combination will always have happened, and will always be part of your score. The past is always a part of every present.

How can one be a good player at this game? What distinguishes the good from the bad players? "The bad player counts on several throws of the dice, on a great number of throws. In this way he makes use of causality and probability to produce a combination that he sees as desirable. He posits this combination itself as an end to be obtained, hidden behind causality."[53] Bad players deny chance. They seek a particular combination, and hope that the throw of the dice will offer it to them. Sevens, not snake eyes. There is an identity, a particular identity or identities, they are awaiting. They will be disappointed if that identity does not turn up. They are working within the realm of possibility, not virtuality. They are calculating a set of probabilities based on possible combinations. Maybe if they just throw the dice again ...

"But, in this way, all that will ever be obtained are more or less probable relative numbers. That the universe has no purpose, that is has no end to hope for any more than it has causes to be known – this is the certainty necessary to play well."[54] Good players do not count

---

[53] Deleuze, *Nietzsche and Philosophy*, p. 26–7.
[54] Deleuze, *Nietzsche and Philosophy*, p. 27.

on a particular future, do not ask to throw the dice one more time. Good players affirm both chance and necessity. They play not for a particular combination, but with the knowledge that the combinations are infinite, and are not up to them.

We should not think that good players are passive. "Whatever happens; it doesn't matter. Just roll the dice." This is not the stance of good players. Good players play, and play with abandon. But they do not expect anything of the universe. The universe owes them nothing. It is headed nowhere in particular and they have no role to play in it. The universe gives what it gives. Good players do not know what it will give, but they give themselves over to the game, in each throw. They do not measure the combination that falls back against other combinations, against the combination that they wished had fallen back, the one that *should have* fallen back. They throw and play to their limit. Without resentment or guilt about throwing the dice or the combination that falls back.

To affirm is not to take responsibility for, to take on the burden of what is, but to release, to set free what lives. To affirm is to unburden: not to load life with the weight of higher values, but *to create* new values which are those of life, which make life light and active. There is creation, properly speaking, only insofar as we can make use of excess in order to invent new forms of life rather than separating life from what it can do.[55]

To affirm is to experiment, without any assurances about the results of one's experimenting. It is to explore the virtual, rather than to cling to the actual. It is to ask with one's life the question of how one might live.

X

Nietzsche distinguishes between active and reactive forces. He is sometimes understood to distinguish between active and reactive people. But this is a mistake. It is not that some people are active, others reactive. People are confluences of forces, some active, some reactive. In a given person, or a given group, or a given society, or even a given species or historical period, it is uncertain which forces will predominate, the

---

55 Deleuze, *Nietzsche and Philosophy*, p. 185.

active or the reactive. Recall that when Deleuze asks how one might live, the one is not necessarily a person. How might a group live? How might a force live? How might an epoch live?

"Every force which goes to the limit of its power is . . . active."[56] An active force goes to the limit of what it can do. It does whatever is in its power to the extent of its ability. Active forces are creative, because they seek to exercise themselves, to make whatever can be made of themselves. What gets created is not only up to the active force. It also concerns the context in which that force expresses itself and its own ability to reach its limit. The universe does not necessarily cooperate with active forces, which means that their creativity may be channeled in unexpected directions, or even undermined altogether. All creativity is an experiment. One throws the dice, but does not know what will fall back.

Active forces may also be destructive. But this is not because they seek to destroy. In creating, there may be obstacles in the way of active forces, impediments to their going to the limit of what they can do. These may be destroyed by the active force, not out of hatred or malice but out of the joy of going to the limit that active forces are engaged in. What threaten active forces are not other active forces, which can at best only compete with or destroy an active force. What threaten active forces are reactive forces.

Reactive forces "proceed in an entirely different way – they decompose; *they separate active force from what it can do*; they take away a part or almost all of its power."[57] If active forces go to the limit of their power, create through their self-expression, reactive forces operate by cutting active forces off from their own power. Reactive forces do not overcome active forces; they undermine them. They do not create; they stifle the creativity of active forces.

Think of churches and homosexuality. Homosexuality, like hetero-sexuality, is a force. It seeks to express itself. As active force, homosexuality may seek to go to its limit: to find new forms of sexual expression, to express itself with many others (or on the contrary to express itself more deeply with a single other), to ride the crest of its own power. If a particular homosexual force is active, it does not ask itself what other

[56] Deleuze, *Nietzsche and Philosophy*, p. 59.
[57] Deleuze, *Nietzsche and Philosophy*, p. 57.

homosexual forces are doing; it does not wonder what is "proper" for homosexuality; it feels no guilt or remorse or doubt. There is no point to all that.

Nearly all churches, nearly all religions, seek to separate homosexual force from what it can do. Deny it, reject it, threaten it, pity it. The theological relation to homosexuality does not work by going to the limit of what it can do; there is nothing it is seeking to do or to express. It proceeds in an entirely different way. It works by inhibition. Make the homosexual force an outcast. Introduce guilt and punishment. Announce the threat that homosexuality poses for everything around it. It is a relationship that is parasitical upon homosexuality. Without it, there would be no raison d'être for an entire aspect of theological doctrine.

There are many things for which Nietzsche criticized institutional religion. Perhaps none is so trenchant or so profound as the recognition that institutional religion is primarily reactive. It does not operate by allowing forces to go to the limit but by separating them from what they can do, by mobilizing reactive forces against active ones, seeking to render those active forces powerless, guilty, feeble, and finally reactive. The history of institutional religions is a history of populations that define themselves by what they are not, that take their solace not in what they can do but in their not being something else. *"You are evil, therefore I am good."*[58] Weakness parades as virtue, and active forces are numbered among the enemy. "The sick represent the greatest danger for the healthy; it is *not* the strongest but the weakest who spell disaster for the strong. Do we appreciate this?"[59]

People, communities, living beings, epochs – these are combinations of active and reactive forces. (Nietzsche thinks that in our historical period it is the reactive forces that dominate.) We are composed of forces that seek to go the limit of what they can do, and forces that seek to separate those forces from what they can do. Active forces affirm their difference. They do not see themselves through the eyes of others, but instead go to the limit of their own difference. They do not compare; they create. Reactive forces are what they are only through their negation of active forces. Their

[58] Deleuze, *Nietzsche and Philosophy*, p. 119.
[59] Deleuze, *On the Genealogy of Morals*, p. 100.

identity comes not from affirming their difference, from expressing their particular wills, but from negating the differences of the active forces.

Good players of dice affirm active forces. They are not afraid of them. They know that the dice may fail to go to their limit, and that even if they succeed, their effects are as yet unknown. This does not bother them. They affirm both chance and necessity, the difference that is both past and future and the actualization of difference. Good players do not seek to restrict or undermine the creativity of active forces. They leave that for the bad players, the players for whom outcomes must be known in advance and everything arranged to bring those outcomes under control. For the good players themselves, they are aware that they do not even know of what a body is capable; but they are willing to find out.

XI

All of this is a matter of the eternal return. The eternal return is the return of difference. It is the recurrence of pure difference that Bergson shows is the nature of duration. Good players affirm the eternal return. They affirm the return of difference without identity, of differences whose actualization into identities is not a matter of the continuation of rigid forms but instead an experimentation in a world of inexhaustible creative resources. To affirm the eternal return is to recognize a world of virtual difference that lies beyond the particularities of our present, to set free the active forces of creativity, to refuse to separate those forces from what they can do. It is to recognize that the future does not offer us guarantees of what will be there, and moreover that to seek guarantees is to restrict our capacities, to imprison our bodies, to stifle our creative possibilities, to betray what may be the best in us for fear that it may instead be the worst.

The eternal return teaches us that all creativity is an experiment. To affirm our creativity is to open ourselves to the experimentation that the future offers us rather than clinging to the illusory identity that the present places before us. If we are capable of creativity, it is because we are not threatened by the prospect of blazing a path to its limit across a territory that offers no assurances, except that we cannot exhaust its resources. Many, perhaps most in Deleuze's and Nietzsche's eyes, cannot rise to this task. But they do not write for them, but for the few (the few people, the few forces, the few epochs) who can.

Deleuze writes of Nietzsche's concept of the will to power, in contrast to earlier conceptions of the will: "Against this *fettering* of the will Nietzsche announces that willing *liberates*; against the *suffering* of the will Nietzsche announces that the will is *joyful*. Against the image of a will which dreams of having *established* values attributed to it Nietzsche announces that to will is *to create* new values."[60] Liberation, joy, creation. That is what the affirmation of difference, the embrace of the eternal return, amounts to. Not sadness, resentment, pangs of conscience, or self-denial, but their opposite. "Nietzsche's practical teaching is that difference is happy; that multiplicity, becoming and chance are adequate objects of joy by themselves and that only joy returns."[61] And Deleuze asks, as did Nietzsche before him, are we capable of this? Or, to put the question another way, have we the strength to ask how one might live?

XII

Spinoza, Bergson, Nietzsche: Christ, the Father, the Holy Ghost. They create the three concepts that form the tripod on which Deleuze's own philosophy stands: immanence, duration, and the affirmation of difference.

There is one world, one substance, a single being. It is not governed or judged by a world or Being outside it. There is no transcendence. "The idea of another world, of a supersensible world in all its forms (God, essence, the good, truth), the idea of values superior to life, is not one example among many but the constitutive element of all fiction."[62] Being is not something other than the world we live in. It is that world.

This does not mean that there *is* only what is present to us. There is more than meets the eye. Being folds itself, unfolds itself, refolds itself into the specific forms that constitute the world of our experience. Being, or substance, inheres in what presents itself to us, but is

[60] Deleuze, *Nietzsche and Philosophy*, p. 85.
[61] Deleuze, *Nietzsche and Philosophy*, p. 190.
[62] Deleuze, *Nietzsche and Philosophy*, p. 147.

always more than any presentation. To understand this we must think temporally rather than spatially. Spatial thinking can give us only the phenomenology of our world, the structure of appearances. Temporal thinking can penetrate that world to show us what those appearances might be made of, and how they might become different.

Temporal thinking reveals a thickness of duration, a past that is not simply the absence of a present moment but instead a particular kind of subsistence in the present. Past and present imply one another. Without the present there would be nothing to pass. Without the continued existence of the past the present would not pass. There is only one time.

The present is actuality. The past is virtuality. The past is a realm of virtual differences that exist in the present in actualized form. Actualization does not impoverish the virtuality of difference, the multiplicity of duration. Actualization does not freeze being. Rather, it gives it specific forms, specific modes, that express being without exhausting it. The present always holds more than it seems. It is pregnant with its past, which is also its future.

The past, duration, virtual multiplicity, does not simply trail the present. It comes to meet it. The past recurs. It is the eternal recurrence of difference. Duration, which inheres in the present, is also the future. The present is never simply the forms it presents to us. It is always more than appears. It does not lose the multiplicity that constitutes it. As a result, the present is not a matter of stable forms but of modes of difference; the present has actualized itself in one way and may actualize itself in others. We do not even know what a body is capable of. The future, then, is not simply a continuation of the stable forms of the present, since the present is not merely a set of stable forms. The future is unactualized difference, both coming to meet us and already with us.

We can allow ourselves to draw near this difference, to affirm it, to embrace the chance that it is and the necessity that its actualizations will present us with. We can ask what a body is capable of, how one might live. We can ask it not only as human beings, but as groups in action, as products of a historical epoch or environment, as forces that interact with other forces in relations of solidarity, domination, mutual excess.

If we ask, if we permit the question to resonate, then we are open to the creativity of what constitutes us. We allow what is in us or what we are or what we are a part of to seek its limit, to express itself. We do not compare ourselves to what seems to be there now or what has gone before; we experiment with what can be. If, alternatively, we refuse the question, if we refuse to ask how one might live, then we will seek comfort in established values, transcendent beings, judges of all sorts who will take our power from us and hand it back to us in the form of quiescence. We will not seek to discover what we are capable of but instead seek to separate ourselves from what we might be capable of.

In the mainstream of philosophy, the project of ontology has always been to engage in this separation of ourselves from what we might be capable of. Only at the margins have there been figures that have offered a different vision. Spinoza, Bergson, and Nietzsche are among them, presenting us with concepts from which we might build a new ontology, one that does not reinforce a tired conformism but points the way toward a more open, vibrant conception of the world and of living in it.

For Deleuze, to conceive living is to conceive both what is and what might be. It is to offer an account of what it is for something to be living and an opening onto ways to live. In an ontology worthy of the name, the two are entwined. The world is more than we may realize. It is rich with difference. And in this more, in this difference, in the world's ontological constitution, lie responses to the question of how one might live. Or better, since the responses have not yet been formulated, since they are not lying there ready-made and awaiting our embrace, we might say that it is in asking, not only with our words but with our lives, the question of how one might live that responses are formed.

3

Thought, Science, and Language

I

How we think about our world and how we live in it are entwined. Our ontology and our practical engagements are woven together. This is true not only for philosophers. It is true for everyone. A world that consists of particular things with strict borders that interact with other particular things (with *their* strict borders) according to particular natural laws will call us to certain kinds of living. For instance, if particular things are what they are and nothing else, then we will not waste our time imagining what else they might be or might become. We will conform ourselves to the possibilities presented to us by their actuality. We will have to discover the natural laws that relate these particular things to one another so that we do not attempt futilely to break them. We will conform ourselves to these laws just as we conform ourselves to the identities of the things these laws govern.

If we abandon this way of thinking of our world, then alternative ways of living may appear to us. If things don't have strict borders of identity and if the relations among them are not reducible to natural laws, then we can no longer be sure of what a body is capable. Perhaps there is more going on in our world than is presented to us. We don't know. The only way to find out is to experiment.

Immanence, duration, affirmation of difference. These are concepts through which the world becomes strange to us again, through which the borders between things become porous and their identities fluid. To think this way requires a new ontology. But it requires more than that. It requires that we see our old way of thinking for what it is, that we understand its shape and its design. Deleuze calls this old way of thinking the "dogmatic image of thought."

Once we understand the dogmatic image of thought, we will be better able to grasp the new type of thought that Deleuze offers us, a new type of thought, with new concepts that open up new ways of living. This new type of thought will conceive the world differently from the dogmatic image. We should not be misled by its novelty, however. There are those working in the sciences who conceive the world in ways that are not foreign to the way Deleuze conceives it. Science may not verify Deleuze's ontology; philosophy is not the same thing, after all, as science. Philosophy creates concepts. It is concerned not with the truth but with the remarkable, the interesting, and the important. But there are concepts and discoveries in science that may help to illustrate the ontology Deleuze constructs. A new type of science and a new type of philosophy converge on a new conception of the world and the universe in which we live: a world and a universe that may be more alive than we have been led to think.

Our thought and our science are constructed in language. That does not mean that they are simply devices of language, or that there is nothing outside language that has a bearing on us. We are not alone with our language. The perspective Deleuze constructs should have already made that clear. The world contains more than our words can reveal to us, not less. But if our language is not all there is, if the world is not simply woven from our words, then neither is our language distant from us. To understand our conceptions of the world, we must understand the workings of the language in which those conceptions are rendered. A reflection on thought and science, in order to be complete, requires as well a reflection on language.

Thought, science, and language. If immanence, duration, and the affirmation of difference are the concepts that we need to conceive the world anew, then thought, science, and language are the mediums of that new conception. We must abandon the dogmatic image of thought for a new type of thought; we must see that thought more clearly, in ways that science will assist us with; and we must reconsider the language in which all that new type of thought appears.

II

What is the dogmatic image of thought? It is not the possession of a few philosophers, ensconced in their offices, alone with their ideas. Nor is it a treatise to be found in a dusty library, an arcane or secret program that has been passed down the generations in some sort of intellectual conspiracy. The dogmatic image of thought is ours. It is our template for conceiving the world.

Perhaps the most central element of this template is representation. This is how it works. The world is out there, stable and serene. In order to be conceived, it awaits our thought. Our thought represents it. That is what thought does. It mirrors what is there, in its stability and its serenity, in our ideas. Thought is nothing more than a representation of the world: a *re-presentation* in our mind of what is *presented* to us once, already, out there.

This is a simple story, and a compelling one. In ancient thought, there were problems to overcome in making the story plausible. For instance, how can something as big as a cow fit into my mind? Now we think of such problems as silly. This is not because we have overcome representation as the way we think about our thought. Rather, it is because we have been able to refine the template to accommodate potential problems like this. It is not that a cow actually appears in our thought. Rather, our eyes process the image: they pass that image through the optic nerves to the brain, which stores the image and relates it to other images of the same kind, those that fall into the category of "cow."

That is not the only way to tell the story, but the other ways are like it, and they share something it is easy to overlook. At each point there is stability. The image of the cow, the passing and storing of it, the category into which it falls: all these retain the integrity of strict borders, clearly marked boundaries. "Representation," Deleuze says, "fails to capture the affirmed world of difference. Representation has only a single centre, a unique and receding perspective, and in consequence a false depth. It mediates everything, but mobilises and moves nothing."[1]

---

[1] Deleuze, *Difference and Repetition*, p. 55–6.

Representation mediates everything, but mobilizes and moves nothing. We await a thought that mobilizes and moves. Deleuze will try to offer that to us. For now we must understand how the dogmatic image of thought mediates without moving. It does so through the stability of presentation and representation.

At each point, what is there is what there is, and there is nothing else. The cow is a cow and nothing else. Its image is the image of that cow and nothing else. The category is that of "cow" and nothing else. And at every point, what is passed along is what is there and nothing else. That is how representation works. If it did not work that way, it would not be a re-presentation. It would not present again in thought and language what is already there in the world.

Representation is in alliance with truth, or at least a certain conception of truth. There have been several conceptions of truth throughout the history of philosophy. The most important, the one that has dug its roots the deepest into the soil of our thought, is the correspondence view of truth. On this view, a statement is true if it corresponds to the state of affairs about which it is making its claim. The statement "The cow is in the meadow" is true if and only if the cow being referred to is indeed in the meadow being referred to. This seems obviously right. After all, how could the statement "The cow is in the meadow" be true if said cow was not in said meadow (and let us not even begin to consider the possibility that there is no cow there, or that the cow in the meadow is not really a cow but an inanimate model of a cow)?

What is obviously right, though, may be so only within the parameters of a certain image of thought: the dogmatic image. Without this image, the correspondence theory of truth does not have a foothold. What this view of truth requires are all the integrities of representation: integrities of cows and images and nerve passages and categories of language. There can be no correspondence of two elements (the language of the statement and the world of the cow) without each of these having a stability that allows one to reflect the other.

Let us consider, though, the possibility that what is out there in the meadow is not simply a cow, but more than a cow. Let us consider the possibility that cows are more than cows. And, on the other side of the coin, perhaps thought and language are more than a set of stable categories with appropriate functions for navigating through them (pronouns, conjunctions, and so on). Perhaps language bleeds internally, so that no category is as stable as it appears, or, better, that the idea of a "category" does not capture what is going on in language. It may be that there is a chaos internal to both the world and language that undermines the stability of the dogmatic image of thought.

In that case, there would be no representation and no truth, at least no truth as correspondence. Or, more accurately, there might be representation and truth, but there would be more, much more, to which a commitment to representation and truth would blind us. Conceiving that "more" would require something other than the dogmatic image of thought. It would require another image, another thought. Or, better, it would require a thought that no longer involves images: a thought of difference.

Deleuze says that the dogmatic image of thought, thought as representation, operates with what he calls *common sense* and *good sense*:

judgement has precisely two essential functions, and only two: distribution, which it ensures by the *partition* of concepts; and hierarchization, which it ensures by the *measuring* of subjects. To the former corresponds the faculty of judgement known as common sense; to the latter the faculty known as good sense (or first sense). Both constitute just measure or "justice" as a value of judgement. In this sense, every philosophy of categories takes judgement for its model.[2]

Deleuze does not choose the terms *common sense* and *good sense* arbitrarily. They have resonance for us. Common sense: that is what everyone who can navigate their way through life with a minimum of success possesses. To have common sense is to be able to recognize what is obvious. (We will return to the idea of recognition in a bit.) Good sense: that is what everyone with good intuitions has. To have good sense is to know one's way around what is there. These are not the meanings Deleuze gives to the terms; but he is aware of the connotations they possess.

Deleuze finds common sense and good sense in all philosophies of categories, all philosophies of representation. He finds it in Plato and in Aristotle, in Kant and in Hegel. But common sense and good sense are not only to be discovered among philosophers. They are our

---

[2] Deleuze, *Difference and Repetition*, p. 33.

heritage and our thought. The dogmatic image of thought, which is *our* thought, judges by means of common sense and good sense.

In the technical meaning Deleuze ascribes to it, common sense assures the harmony of different mental faculties in judgment of the object. "That cow I'm seeing, and thinking, and saying: it's all the same cow. What's out there is the thing in my mind, and it's the same thing in the different activities (perceptual, cognitive, linguistic) in my mind." Common sense coordinates. It assures me that there is a match between what is inside me and what is outside me, and among the various faculties inside me by means of which I approach what is outside me. "Common sense [is] defined subjectively by the supposed identity of a Self which provided the unity and ground of all the faculties, and objectively by the identity of whatever object served as a focus for all the faculties."[3] That is the distribution Deleuze speaks of: different activities, but the same object and the same subject (me) confronting the object.

But coordination by itself is empty. There has to be some content to be coordinated. There has to be a cow or a meadow that is coordinated between inside and outside and among the faculties of the inside. And the I or the me that coordinates them has to be a particular I or me, not some general or universal one. That is the role that good sense plays. "Common sense must therefore point beyond itself towards another, dynamic instance, capable of determining the indeterminate object as this or that, and of individualising the self situated in this ensemble of objects. This other instance is good sense."[4]

Good sense gives each object its measure; it provides the categories that common sense coordinates. Common sense assures that those categories do not leak, that they are properly matched, one with another. Good sense and common sense converge in providing stability to thought. Good sense does differentiate among objects; it finds that one object is not like another. But it does not do so by engaging the difference that Nietzsche affirms. It does so by means of creating stable categories for each. In this way, difference is subordinated to identity. Things are different because they fall into different categories. They are different precisely in *not being identical or the same*. It is on the

3 Deleuze, *Difference and Repetition*, p. 226.
4 Deleuze, *Difference and Repetition*, p. 226.

basis of the identity of the categories that difference is recognized. The stability of the categories is thereby retained. The integrities of the dogmatic image of thought are assured.

Common sense reinforces that stability. There are different faculties inside me, and what is outside me is different from me. But there is co-ordination among these differences, which in the end yields identity. Not an identity that emerges out of differences, but an identity that is their very operation. Nothing escapes the categories or their co-ordination. Nothing leaks out. There is nothing left over. Everything fits.

The coordination of common sense and good sense offers us a model of judgment as *recognition*. To judge is to recognize. Why is this? To judge is to take the material of our experience and to fit it into categories that we already possess. It is to apply a category that will assure the coordination of experience among the different faculties (perception, cognition, language, and so on). When we make a judg-ment, it is always through a recognition of what is there, a fitting of what is there into representational categories that we already possess.

This does not mean that judgment is always of one type. Judgement, in Deleuze's view (borrowing from Aristotle), can be of four different types: identity, analogy, opposition, or resemblance.

Identity: x equals y; x is the same thing as y.
Analogy: x shares a quality with y.
Opposition: x is opposed to y or x is not y.
Resemblance: x is like y.

To perform any of these judgments requires that we already have an x or a y available to us. And it requires not only that they are available to us, but also that the x and the y be the very categories through which judgment happens. They are the *basis* for judgment. This, in turn, requires that there be a stability of judging that allows x to remain x in all circumstances, and y to remain y. Common sense and good sense provide that stability. Identity, analogy, opposition, and resemblance are the operations of a judgment structured by common sense and good sense. They are the elements of the representational or dogmatic image of thought. And they are the means by which we conceive our world, the means by which we recognize it.

What is that? (A question of recognition.) *It looks like a cow.* (Resemblance, supported by the categories of good sense.) *I remember what cows look like.* (Common sense.) *It surely isn't a steer; they have horns.* (Opposition.) *It has hooves like a steer, though.* (Analogy.) *But it's a cow. In fact, it's the same cow I saw in that meadow yesterday.* (Identity.)

The dogmatic image of thought: the ether of our conception of the world. But what is wrong with it? Is there a problem here? We think about the world in the categories our language presents to us, representing it in the stability it presents to us and carrying that stability throughout the process from perception to conception. What could be wrong with that?

There is a problem. "Philosophy is left without means to realise its project of breaking with *doxa*."[5] *Doxa* is opinion. It is what everybody knows, or what everybody should know. It is common sense and good sense, both in the more everyday meaning of those terms and in the more technical sense Deleuze constructs. The dogmatic image of thought may allow philosophy to challenge a particular *doxa*. But it still operates within the structure of *doxa*. It never leaves the arena of common opinion; it is always within a realm that is already familiar to us.

There is a deep conformism of thought here.

It is surprising, although less remarked upon than it should be, that ethical theories in philosophy so often reinforce common moral opinion, no matter how far their theoretical journeys stray from mundane experience. Kant, for instance, takes ethics on a journey to universal reason. He revisits the nature of our freedom, plumbs the depths of our subjectivity, asks after the role of God. And yet, many of the ethical recommendations that emerge from this journey are uncontroversial, even pedestrian. The moral impermissibility of lying, the sanctions against suicide and cheating one's neighbor, while based in a thought that has gone to far places, do not invite us to strange adventures of our own.[6]

---

5 Deleuze, *Difference and Repetition*, p. 134.

6 Deleuze thinks that Kant is capable of stranger adventures than his ethical recommendations would lead one to believe. In his slim volume on Kant, he uses the Third Critique to open up a realm of chaos that one would not normally associate with Kantian thought. See Deleuze, *Kant's Critical Philosophy: The Doctrine of the Faculties*.

This is *doxa*, Deleuze would say, pure *doxa*. "What," he asks, "is a thought which harms no one, neither thinkers nor anyone else? Recognition is a sign of the celebration of monstrous nuptials, in which thought 'rediscovers' the State, rediscovers 'the Church' and rediscovers all the current values that it subtly presented in the pure form of an eternally blessed unspecified eternal object."[7] The problem is not with Kant, nor specifically with any other philosopher. The problem is with the structure of the thought that underlies their philosophies, the dogmatic image of thought itself. If we are to loosen the chains that have bound our thought, and the thought of most of the history of philosophy, then we must learn to think differently, to abandon representational thought for something else. We must embark in unfamiliar crafts to uncharted territory.

It has been done before. Spinoza did it, as did Nietzsche and Bergson. As Deleuze notes:

here and there isolated and passionate cries are raised. How could they not be isolated when they deny what "everybody knows . . ."? And passionate, since they deny that which, it is said, nobody can deny? Such protest does not take place in the name of aristocratic prejudices; it is not a question of saying what few think and knowing what it means to think. On the contrary, it is a question of someone – if only one – with the necessary modesty not managing to know what everybody knows.[8]

For Foucault and for Derrida, not managing to know what everybody knows requires the abandonment of ontology. It is ontology that gives us the categories of recognition, the content of our representational thought. And it is only by abandoning ontology, either by recounting the contingent history of its most unassailable concepts or by showing the reliance of those concepts on what they are meant to deny, that we can manage to forget what everybody knows. To embark on strange adventures, to leave behind the question of how one should live or what one must do, to embrace instead the question of how one might live, to do these things requires that we cast adrift not merely from this or that ontology but from ontology altogether. We cannot surmount the dogmatic image of thought unless we are prepared to jettison the ontology that supports it.

---

[7] Deleuze, *Difference and Repetition*, pp. 135–6.
[8] Deleuze, *Difference and Repetition*, p. 130.

Deleuze does not agree. Ontology itself has strange adventures in store for us, if only we can think differently about how it might be conceived. If we stop searching for the true, stop asking the world to allow us to recognize it, stop knowing what everybody knows, then we can set off on a new thought, a thought that is both ontological and foreign, an experiment in ontology, rather than an exercise in dogmatism. "Philosophy does not consist in knowing and is not inspired by truth. Rather, it is categories like Interesting, Remarkable, or Important that determine its success or failure. Now, this cannot happen before being constructed."[9]

III

Suppose we consider the possibility that there is more to our world than we can perceive, and more than we can conceive. Suppose the world overflows the categories of representation that the dogmatic image of thought imposes upon it. This is not to say that our particular categories are lacking something that other, better categories would give us. Our imagination must go further than that. We need to consider the possibility that the world (or, since the concept of the world is too narrow, things or being or what there is) outruns any categories we might seek to use to capture it. We will see in the next section, when we discuss science, that we have some reason to think that this possibility is in fact true.[10] But for now let us just consider the possibility.

One way to think about this would be to say that being is difference, that beneath the identities that the dogmatic image of thought offers to us is a realm of pure difference, irreducible to any identity: "difference is behind everything, but behind difference there is nothing."[11]

What might this mean? We need to be careful here. Deleuze may seem to be moving back into representational thought. It could look as though he were merely substituting one concept for another. It's not identity that captures what things are; it's difference that does it. To read him that way would be to keep his thought circulating within the

9 Deleuze and Guattari, *What Is Philosophy?*, p. 82.
10 Although we must always bear in mind that it is not truth Deleuze seeks. Science, then, may illustrate his thought, but science cannot provide either confirmation or disconfirmation.
11 Deleuze, *Difference and Repetition*, p. 57.

dogmatic image. For Deleuze, to say that being is difference is not at all like saying that being is identity (or identities), and not simply because he is saying that it is really something else. The term "difference" is not another concept designed to capture the nature of being or the essence of what there is. It is a term he uses to refer to that which eludes such capture.

In order to follow Deleuze's thought here we must ask what the term "difference" seeks to palpate, not what it seeks to represent. And even then we are in dangerous waters, because if we give an answer to that *what* in representational terms, we are back in the dogmatic image. The term "difference" palpates what it cannot conceive; it gestures at what it cannot grasp. We experience the actualities difference presents us with, but must think the difference that yields them. We might say that difference is the overflowing character of things themselves, their inability to be wrestled into categories of representation. If we say this, however, we must again be careful. There is no strategy of resistance among things. Being is not bothered when it is represented. Rather, being is always more and therefore other than what representation posits for it. The world (or what there is) is in its very character a transgression of the categories of any representational thought; it is an offense to both good sense and common sense. These latter merely capture the surface of things. In doing so, they both betray what we might say there is and reinforce the deathly conformity of *doxa*.

Behind the identities the dogmatic image of thought presents to us, difference is what there is. This difference may be virtual, but it is not transcendent. It is there, coiled in the heart of things. It is of their very nature. When Deleuze says that difference is behind everything, we should not take him to mean that it is *beyond* everything. It is behind things, but still within them. "Being is said in a single and same sense of everything of which it is said, but that of which it is said differs: it is said of difference itself."[12] This, of course, is the lesson of Spinoza's immanence.

One way to approach the thought of difference would be, as Deleuze does, to think of being as a problem, and to seek a prob- lematizing thought that can follow its contours. We often think badly about problems; either that or we think about bad or uninteresting

---

[12] Deleuze, *Difference and Repetition*, p. 36.

problems. When we think about problems, we tend to think about them in terms of solutions. Problems, it seems to us, seek solutions. Not only do they seek solutions, each problem seeks a unique solution, or at least a small set of them. It is as though a problem were merely a particular lack or fault that a solution will fill or rectify. That is how we were taught to think of problems at school. And that is why schools have so many tests. Tests propose problems in order to see whether you know the solution. It is the solution that matters, not the problem. "We are led to believe that problems are given ready-made, and that they disappear in the responses or the solution. . . . We are led to believe that the activity of thinking . . . begins only with the search for solutions."[13]

Here are some examples of this way of thinking about problems:

1. How much is two plus two?
2. What is the fastest route from here to the grocery store?
3. What was the crucial mistake that Napoleon made in Russia that cost him the war there?
4. Who were the most popular jazz performers of the past decade?

These are problems that seek solutions, problems whose character is defined by the fact that there are particular solutions they seek. Here are a couple of problems that might look like the first four, but are not, or at least do not need to be:

1. How did the dodo bird come to appear on the planet?
2. Is Nietzsche's philosophy relevant to us today?

We can, of course, approach these problems in the way we approach the first four. We might answer the first question by reference to genetic mutations the dodo bird instantiated and why, at that time, those genetic mutations were adaptive. But we do not need to approach things this way. Instead of seeing these as problems that seek a particular solution, we might see them as opening up fields of discussion, in which there are many possible solutions, each of which captures something, but not everything, put before us by the problem.

Take the case of the dodo bird. Instead of accounting for its emergence in terms of particular mutations and environmental niches, we

---

[13] Deleuze, *Difference and Repetition*, p. 158.

might look more holistically at the environment. We might say that the environment itself is a problem, one that lends itself to many solutions. The dodo bird was a solution to that problem, although perhaps not the only one. Another solution might have been a change of vegetation, or another kind of animal that mutated from another species but fed on similar products. Or we might look at the matter differently, from the point of view of populations. The relation of the species of bird from which the dodo bird comes to the environmental niche that species occupied was a problem. The population of that species fit into that niche in a certain way. There were perhaps other types of fit. Through the accident of a genetic mutation, the dodo bird offered another solution to the problem of how that population fit into that niche. It was a solution that occurred alongside the solution that the original species formed or instead of it, depending on environmental conditions.

If we look at things this way, we are no longer looking at problems in terms of solutions. Problems become an open field in which a variety of solutions may take place. It is the problems rather than the solutions that are primary. Thinking of being as difference is an example of a problematizing rather than a representational thought. "Being (what Plato calls the Idea) 'corresponds' to the essence of the problem or the question as such. It is as though there were an 'opening', a 'gap', an ontological 'fold' which relates being and the question to one another. In this relation, being is difference itself."[14]

Taking being as difference is a problematizing rather than a dogmatic approach to ontology. Contrast this approach to the dogmatic approach. For dogmatism, there are stable entities that can be represented through stable categories. There is, as we saw, stability at every stage. This does not mean that there has to be only one answer to every problem or only one way for identities or thoughts to combine. But in each case, the answers or combinations are constructed out of discrete elements, which in turn form other discrete things or ideas when they combine. The elements are limited to "what everybody knows," and thus their combinations will not stretch much beyond "what everybody knows," if they stretch at all.

---

[14] Deleuze, *Difference and Repetition*, p. 64.

For Deleuze, this is a case of the solution defining the problem. To see why, recall the relation of the virtual to the actual. The virtual is not the same as the actual; it has a different character. Solutions are actual; problems are virtual. The dodo bird is an actual solution to the problem of a particular environment. Solutions present themselves as stable identities whereas problems (at least the worthwhile ones) present themselves as "open fields" or "gaps" or "ontological folds." Problems are inexhaustible, while solutions are a particular form of exhaustion.[15]

For the dogmatic image of thought, being is defined in terms of actuality rather than virtuality. It is a matter of stable identities rather than difference. To think ontologically in terms of stable identities is to read solutions back into problems, to approach problems in terms of solutions. For Deleuze, being is not a matter of the stable identities that representational thought gives us. Identities come later, as particular solutions to the problems that being places before us, the problem that being is. To confuse those identities with being is to confuse the actual with the virtual. It is to confuse solutions and problems. The dogmatic image of thought gives primacy to identities, to the actual and solutions. It sees difference in terms of these.

If these are the terms of ontology, no wonder Foucault and Derrida abandon the project of ontology. The other course, the one Deleuze takes, is to set ontology on another path, the path of being as difference.

It is what Deleuze thinks any good philosophy must do. In his first book, on the philosopher David Hume, he writes, that

a philosophical theory is an elaborately developed question, and nothing else; by itself and in itself, it is not the resolution to a problem, but the elaboration, *to the very end*, of the necessary implications of a formulated question. . . . In

---

[15] This does not mean that solutions do not carry particular problems within them. The virtual remains within the actual. "A problem does not exist, apart from its solutions. Far from disappearing in this overlay, however, it insists and persists in these solutions." Deleuze, *Difference and Repetition*, p. 163. But inasmuch as we call something a solution, we are seeing it in terms of its actuality rather than its virtuality. The dodo bird may be more than merely a dodo bird, but it is also a dodo bird, and as such is a particular solution. As such, it is a way of addressing a particular problem.

philosophy, the question and the critique of the question are one; or, if you wish, there is no critique of solutions, there are only critiques of problems.[16]

This is why the issue of truth does not matter to Deleuze, why it is the remarkable, the interesting, and the important that matter. And this is why, in Deleuze's hands, ontology is not a matter of telling us what there is but of taking us on strange adventures, bringing us far afield of ourselves. Finally, this is why philosophy is a project of not managing to know what everybody knows.

Teachers already know that errors or falsehoods are rarely found in home-work (except in those exercises where a fixed result must be produced, or propositions must be translated one by one). Rather, what is more frequently found – and worse – are nonsensical sentences, remarks without interest or importance, banalities mistaken for profundities . . . badly posed or distorted problems – all heavy with dangers, yet the fate of us all. . . . Philosophy must draw the conclusions which follow from this.[17]

IV

It is not only philosophy that can think difference. Science can do it too. There are scientists whose work offers a context for thinking of being as difference, for thinking the world as a problematic field or set of problematic fields in which actual biological or chemical entities are particular solutions. As discussed earlier, thinking of being as difference might be not only a divergent form of thought from the dogmatic image, but also a more adequate approach to what there is and to how things are than the dogmatic image offers. It is possible that the world does in fact overflow the categories we use to try to capture it, and that it may overflow *any* categories whose goal is its capture.

Several areas in science, particularly in biology and in chemistry, offer examples of this. The approach in these areas of science is no longer as a project of seeking laws governing stable identities, which was the way we all learned in high school that science was supposed to be approached, the way Newton approached the inertia governing moving and stable bodies or Galileo the study of falling bodies. Instead,

---

[16] Deleuze, *Empiricism and Subjectivity*, p. 106.
[17] Deleuze, *Difference and Repetition*, p. 153.

science is seen as a matter of understanding systems of differences in dynamic relation.

Biologists have largely moved away from seeing life as a matter of living beings and toward a view of biological and ecological systems. The living being is not necessarily the primary unit of biological study; instead, life or the environment is. One of the thinkers who most influenced Deleuze's *Difference and Repetition*, Gilbert Simondon, has put it this way:

> the individual is to be understood as having a relative reality, occupying only a certain phase of the whole being in question – a phase that therefore carries the implication of a preceding preindividual state, and that, even after individuation, does not exist in isolation, since individuation does not exhaust in the single act of its appearance all the potentials embedded in the preindividual state.[18]

The preindividual state, the state of biological being, is not exhausted by the actuality of any given individual. There is always more than meets the eye.

Simondon's idea of a preindividual state recognizes the significance of the virtual as a field of difference, or, as Deleuze sometimes calls it, a field of intensities. "The expression 'difference of intensity' is a tautology," Deleuze says. "Intensity is the form of difference in so far as this is the reason of the sensible."[19] We might think of intensities in contrast to "extensities." Extensities exist in the actual realm, intensities in the virtual realm. Intensities are relations of difference that give rise to the extensive world, the actual world, but are not directly accessible to perception in the actual world. "Intensity is difference, but this difference tends to deny or cancel itself out in extensity and underneath quality."[20]

What does Deleuze see Simondon as proposing? The biological individual is an actualization of a virtual intensive state, one that does not exhaust the potential of the virtual but that brings it into a specific

---

[18] Simondon, "The Genesis of the Individual," p. 300. This text is the introduction to Simondon's *L'individu et sa genèse physico-biologique*, Paris: Presses Universitaires de France, 1964.

[19] Deleuze, *Difference and Repetition*, p. 221.

[20] Deleuze, *Difference and Repetition*, p. 222.

actualization. Deleuze describes Simondon's contribution:

Individuation emerges like the act of solving a problem, or – what amounts to the same thing – like the actualization of a potential and the establishing of communication between disparates.... Individuation is the act by which intensity determines differential relations to become actualised, along the lines of differenciation and within the qualities and extensities it creates.[21]

The individuation of a biological creature is an actualization of virtual difference, a solving of a problem. We have seen that this does not eliminate the problem; the ontological field remains. A biological individual is a solution *within* the problem.

There are examples of this. Think of a gene not as a set of discrete bits of information but instead as part of a virtual field of intensities that actualizes into specific concrete beings. The gene is not a closed system of pregiven information that issues out directly into individual characteristics. Instead, the genetic code is in constant interaction with a field of variables that in their intensive interaction generate a specific living being. The environmentalist Barry Commoner has argued that the failure to recognize this point is what leads to the dangers of genetic engineering, since genetic engineering as it is practiced assumes that the introduction of a gene into a foreign body will result in the passing on of that gene's information without alteration or remainder. That assumption has been shown to be empirically false, with fatal results, and, if practiced widely, would be potentially disastrous.[22] We must conceive of genetic passage, then, not as the perpetuation of individuals by means of a closed genetic code, but rather as the unfolding of a genetic virtuality that has among its products the individuation of organisms, the creation of biological individuals. Or, as Simondon puts the point, "the being contains not only that which is identical to itself, with the result that being qua being – previous to any individuation – can be grasped as something more than a unity and more than an identity," adding that "This method presupposes a postulate of an ontological nature."[23]

It is the last phrase that suggests something no longer biological, but philosophical. What is required is a new ontology, no longer in thrall

---

[21] Deleuze, *Difference and Repetition*, p. 246.
[22] Barry Commoner, "Unraveling the DNA Myth," pp. 39–47.
[23] Simondon, "The Genesis of the Individual," p. 312.

to the dogmatic image of thought. A new way of conceiving being, not in terms of identities but in terms of difference or, as he sometimes puts it, multiplicities.

When and under what conditions should we speak of a multiplicity? There are three conditions... (1) the elements of the multiplicity must have neither sensible form nor conceptual signification.... They are not even actually existent, but inseparable from a potential or a virtuality. In this sense they imply no prior identity.... (2) These elements must in effect be determined, but reciprocally, by reciprocal relations which allow no independence whatsoever to subsist.... (3) A multiple ideal connection, a differential *relation* must be actualized in diverse spatio-temporal *relationships*, at the same time as its *elements* are actually incarnated in a variety of *terms* and forms.[24]

Simondon's preindividual state is an example of a multiplicity. Its elements are not conceivable in terms of identity; they are not representable. They are, as Barry Commoner points out, reciprocally determined. And they issue out into particular individuals.

Another example is that of an egg. Deleuze writes that,

Individuating difference must be understood first within its field of individuation – not as belated, but as in some sense in the egg. Since the work of Child and Weiss, we recognize axes or planes of symmetry within an egg. Here, too, however, the positive element lies less in the elements of the given symmetry than in those which are missing. An intensity forming a wave of variation throughout the protoplasm distributes its difference along the axes and from one pole to another.... the individual in the egg is a genuine descent, going from the highest to the lowest and affirming the differences which comprise it and in which it falls.[25]

The egg is a field of differential intensities, a preindividual field from within which an individual arises. We should not think of the egg as a biological being in germ. It is different in kind from the individual that emerges from it (the virtual is different in kind from the actual); because of this, there is something that overflows the biological individual.

The philosopher Keith Ansell Pearson remarks that Deleuze's use of Simondon implies that "it is the process itself that is to be regarded as primary. This means that ontogenesis is no longer treated as dealing

---

[24] Deleuze, *Difference and Repetition*, p. 183.
[25] Deleuze, *Difference and Repetition*, p. 250.

with the genesis of the individual but rather designates the becoming of being."[26] Bergson and Spinoza are the touchstones here. Bergson's concept of duration offers the framework for understanding the process of the unfolding of difference as the actualization of the virtual. Spinoza's concept of the univocity of being reveals this process as an immanent unfolding, an expression, rather than a transcendent creation or emanation.

In his turn, Deleuze takes Simondon's framework and generalizes it to the unfolding of the world itself, going beyond the biological to the ontological. He writes:

> The world is an egg.... We think that difference in intensity, as this is implicated in the egg, expresses first the differential relations or virtual matter to be organized. This intensive field of individuation determines the relations that it expresses to be incarnated in spatio-temporal dynamisms (dramatisation), in species which correspond to these relations (specific differenciation), and in organic parts which correspond to the distinctive points in these relations (organic differenciation).[27]

V

It is not only Simondon who views biology in terms of ontological difference. When Deleuze starts his collaboration with Felix Guattari, he refers to the work of the biochemist Jacques Monod. *Anti-Oedipus*, published in 1972, two years after Monod's seminal *Chance and Necessity*,[28] adopts Monod's treatment of biological enzymes as having "cognitive" properties, allowing for the combination of disparate elements into new life forms. Monod articulates that idea in a way that converges with Simondon's earlier work on biological individuation.

Chance and Necessity is famous chiefly for its conclusion that human beings are the product of biological chance rather than any form of evolutionary necessity. But it is not exclusively Monod's conclusion that interests Deleuze and Guattari. It is also the chemical analysis on which he bases his conclusion. Monod analyzes particular enzymes, and especially a class of enzymes known as "allosteric" enzymes, which

---

[26] Pearson, *Germinal Life: The Difference and Repetition of Deleuze*, p. 90.
[27] Deleuze, *Difference and Repetition*, p. 251.
[28] Monod, *Chance and Necessity: An Essay on the Natural Philosophy of Modern Biology*.

not only perform the function of binding chemical substrates, but can also regulate their own activity on the basis of the existence of other compounds. Monod says that allosteric enzymes "have the further property of recognizing electively one or several *other* compounds, whose . . . association with the protein has a modifying effect – that is, depending on the case, of *heightening or inhibiting its activity with respect to the substrate.*"[29] Monod calls this property a "cognitive" one. It means that there is a process of self-ordering at the molecular level that does not require the intervention of an already constituted highly ordered system. The allosteric enzyme recognizes and responds to its environmental conditions.

The emergence of complex biological systems arises from a group of molecular interactions that require nothing more than the right opportunity provided by chance mixings in order to develop into those systems. "Order, structural differentiation, acquisition of functions – all these appear out of a random mixture of molecules individually devoid of any activity, any intrinsic functional capacity other than that of recognizing the partners with which they will build the structure."[30]

Given this approach to molecular biology, the rise of human beings would be more a matter of chance than necessity. Better, it would be a combination of chance and necessity. The fortuitous meeting of certain enzymes under certain conditions facilitate the formation of specific types of biological compounds that give rise to certain life forms. Whether those life forms are reproduced depends on the capacity for those compounds to thrive in a given environment. That those life forms would eventuate in human life is a random matter. That is what interests Monod.

A different lesson interests Deleuze and Guattari even more. Allosteric and other types of enzymes contain the capacity for all sorts of combinations at the preindividual level. Moreover, these combinations, because they are the product of chance, might have been and might become otherwise. The molecular level is a virtual realm of intensities, a field of difference that actualizes itself into specific biological arrangements. As Monod puts the matter, "With the globular protein we already have, at the molecular level, a veritable machine – a

[29] Monod, *Chance and Necessity*, p. 63.
[30] Monod, *Chance and Necessity*, p. 86.

machine in its functional properties, but not, as we now see, in its fundamental structure, where nothing but the play of blind combinations can be discerned. . . . A *totally* blind process can by definition lead to anything; it can even lead to vision itself."[31]

At different levels of biological complexity – Simondon at the level of the gene and its environment, Monod at the level of pre-genetic molecular interaction that leads up to the gene – both these biologists offer a picture of a complex preindividual field that allows for the generation of specific individual forms but also is not bound or reducible to those forms. They posit a field of difference that outruns any specific biological forms or individuals while still giving rise to them. Moreover, since that field is immanent to the physical realm, it requires no movement toward transcendence in order to conceive it. It is a realm of immanent difference, which actualizes itself into particular differences while remaining an ontological fold or gap. It is a problem that actualizes itself in different solutions.

VI

One more set of examples, perhaps the most striking set. In the later collaboration between Deleuze and Guattari, the writings of Ilya Prigogine become increasingly important. Prigogine, whose book *La nouvelle alliance* (co-authored with Isabelle Stengers and partially translated as *Order Out of Chaos*) appeared in 1979, argues for a self-ordering of chemical components into patterns and relationships that cannot be read off from the previous state of chemical disarray. "The artificial," he writes, "may be deterministic and reversible. The natural contains essential elements of randomness and irreversibility. This leads to a new view of matter in which matter is no longer the passive substance described in the mechanistic world view but is associated with spontaneous activity."[32]

---

[31] Monod, *Chance and Necessity*, p. 98.

[32] Prigogine and Stengers, *Order Out of Chaos: Man's New Dialogue with Nature*, p. 9. In this view of matter, the authors show some sympathy for Bergson when they write that "*durée*, Bergson's 'lived time,' refers to the basic dimensions of becoming, the irreversibility that Einstein was willing to admit only at the phenomenological level." p. 294. In the original French edition of this book there are several complimentary references to Deleuze and borrowings from his work that do not appear in the English

Prigogine offers the example of the chemical clock. In conditions that move away from equilibrium (for example, conditions of intense heat or other type of energy), a process they describe with the following image might occur:

Suppose we have two molecules, "red" and "blue." Because of the chaotic motion of the molecules, we would expect that at a given moment we would have more red molecules, say, in the left part of a vessel. Then a bit later more blue molecules would appear, and so on. The vessel would appear to us as "violet," with occasional irregular flashes or red or blue. However, this is *not* what happens with a chemical clock; here the system is all blue, then it abruptly changes its color to red, then again to blue. Because all these changes occur at *regular* time intervals, we have a coherent process.[33]

This is unexpected. It is not the introduction of some sort of ordering mechanism that makes the chemical clock appear. Nothing is brought in from the outside. It is an inherent capability of the chemicals themselves for self-organization that gives rise to this phenomenon. It is as though there were virtual potentialities for communication or coordination contained in the chemicals themselves, or at least in their groupings, that are actualized under conditions that move away from equilibrium.

Prigogine discusses another example that points to the self-organizing of matter: "bifurcations." Bifurcations are situations, once again under conditions far from equilibrium, in which a chemical system will "choose" between two or more possible structures, but which structure it chooses cannot be predicted in advance. It is only a matter of probability, not natural law, which structure will result. Therefore, the resulting structure is not reversible into its initial conditions. One cannot read backwards from what did happen to what was going to happen. Something else might have happened.

edition. For example, the following passage cites *Nietzsche and Philosophy* but could well stand as a summation of *Difference and Repetition*: "Science, which describes the transformations of energy under the sign of equivalence, must admit, however, that only *difference* can produce effects, which would in turn be differences themselves. The conversion of energy is nothing other than the *destruction* of one difference and the *creation* of another." *La Nouvelle Alliance: Métamorphose de la science*, p. 127 (my translation).

[33] Prigogine and Stengers, *Order Out of Chaos*, pp. 147–8.

And there is more. When bifurcation is about to occur, small changes in the surrounding environmental conditions might have large effects on the outcome of the bifurcation. This introduces another element of chance into the understanding of chemistry. "Self-organizing processes in far-from-equilibrium conditions correspond to a delicate interplay between chance and necessity, between fluctuations and deterministic laws. We expect that near a bifurcation, fluctuations or random elements would play an important role, while between bifurcations the deterministic aspects would become dominant."[34]

A delicate interplay between chance and necessity. Monod finds it. Prigogine finds it. It is Nietzsche's dice throw; the dice that are thrown and the dice that fall back. In the realm of science, Monod and Prigogine are among the better players. They understand that there is no being, only becoming. Or, as Deleuze puts it, that the only being is the being of becoming.

The lesson here is not that chemistry is just random. It is that there is a self-ordering process within the chemical realm that cannot be reduced to strict laws because of the capacity of chemicals to combine with and react to disparate chemical elements or physical conditions in new and unpredictable ways. In other words, there is a virtual realm of difference out of which actualizations of diverse elements can appear. At the level of the virtual, the level of pure difference, there is no precluding what will combine with what or what will result. Disparate combinations and unexpected outcomes are the very possibilities of the virtual.

Prigogine and Stengers conclude that *"Nonequilibrium brings 'order out of chaos."*[35] We must be careful to interpret those words in a particular way. This does not mean that when we move from a situation of chaos to one of order, chaos is left behind. Such an understanding would amount to a return to an emanative or creative view of causality. If matter expresses itself in particular organized or self-organized forms, it is not because we have left behind chaos or difference. Organized and self-organized matter brings its chaos along with it, not as actualized but as virtual. Matter preserves its capacity for disparate

---

34 Prigogine and Stengers, *Order Out of Chaos*, p. 176.
35 Prigogine and Stengers, *Order Out of Chaos*, p. 286.

combinations and novel actualizations at every point. The virtual is immanent to matter as both chaotic and organized. Chaos yields order, but it does not yield *to* order; difference does not yield to identity.

Recent scientific approaches offer us Spinoza's immanence, Bergson's duration, Nietzsche's affirmation of difference. They offer us a virtual realm of pure difference, a problematic field in which solutions do not overcome problems but simply actualize them under specific conditions. These discussions cannot be captured by the dogmatic image of thought. Matter and life cannot be represented; their dynamism overflows the stable identities with which representation would seek to shackle them. Whatever we see, whatever we say, there is more – always more.

VII

How can our language say this "more"? Or, if not say it, at least not violate it when it speaks? It seems as though it already has. Over all these many pages, we have addressed a pure difference that resists representation, a difference that emerges in both philosophy and science and that can be palpated but not brought under the categories of the dogmatic image of thought. We have followed Deleuze's construction of an ontology of this difference.

We have done all this in language. That is how philosophy is done, after all. It is done in language. How else might it be done?

But there is a problem here that needs to be confronted. Might it not be that *language itself* is inescapably representational? Might it not be that our words can do no more than represent the world that is presented to us? If that is so, then the very medium of Deleuze's ontology betrays him as he writes, and betrays us as we read him.

We have proceeded all along as though language were transparent. We have proceeded as though words effaced themselves and left us with nothing more or less than the thoughts those words were meant to express. We have discussed Deleuze as though words do just what we want them to do. It is not that we have not recognized the limits to language. After all, a central feature of Deleuze's ontology is that difference can be palpated but not brought into the categories of representation. But what we have done, oddly, is to assume that phrases like *difference can be palpated but not brought into the categories of representation* are themselves transparent. And therein lies the problem. In accepting the working of language uncritically, we have allowed the dogmatic image of thought to slip back into philosophy: not through what we have tried to think, but through the medium through which we try to think it.

Deleuze seeks to overcome the dogmatic image of thought in order to construct an ontology of difference. Central to the dogmatic image of thought is the commitment to language as a representational medium. The stable entities of the world appear to our perception, which in turn carries images of those stable entities to our brain, which in its own turn represents those images in the stable categories of language. Language, then, is a medium that represents the world. It is a transparent medium – it reflects the world as it is, and without remainder.

In rejecting the dogmatic image, Deleuze has offered a view of being that overflows the categories representation seeks to impose on it. The world is always more than representation can capture; the world remains untamed by the dogmatic image of thought.

But what about language itself? If we are to reject the conception of the world offered to us by the dogmatic image of thought, are we also to reject the image of language as seeking to represent that world? The world, being, overflows representational categories. Does language itself also overflow those categories?

If Deleuze's thought is to compel us, it would seem that it must. For if language fails to overflow those categories, then his own thought will be caught in the net of the dogmatic image of thought. After all, if the medium of his thought faithfully reflects the ideas he wants to convey, then we have returned to the stability he seeks to overcome, not at the level of the world he describes but at the level of the language he uses to describe it.

It is not enough to say that we avoid this problem by talking about palpating difference rather than representing it. Because the problem, once again, lies with the words *palpating difference rather than representing it*. What are we doing when we say these words, or when we say any words at all?

The challenge Deleuze confronts is to substitute for the representational view of language a view that allows it to overflow the categories of representation. He needs to construct, alongside his ontology, a view of language adequate to that ontology. Just as he finds a difference in being that resists capture by the stable categories of the dogmatic image of thought, so he must find in the language in which he tells us about this difference something that, equally, resists those stable categories. He must make the language of his ontology resonate with the same irrecuperable energy that he has discovered in the ontology itself. In short, he must offer us what he calls a *logic of sense*.

(One might be tempted to extend the problem yet another turn, twisting it once again. If Deleuze offers a view of language that is in keeping with the ontology he has created, what about the language in which he offers us this view of language? Should we see the language of that view of language as itself an accurate representation of how language works? And, if we do, don't we fall into the same problem, this time at the level of "the language about the language"? Alternatively, if we concede that language itself overflows its representational categories, then does Deleuze's view of language undercut itself? After all, if we cannot represent how language works, then doesn't the language of his view of language also overflow what he wants to say? Is there a dilemma here? No, there isn't. Deleuze can concede that his view of language overflows its representational categories without undercutting himself. He offers us a view of how language works. That view sees language as overflowing its representational categories. There is more than representation can capture. If there is, then the language of his own account of language overflows its representational content. The trembling of language goes all the way up the line, from language to his account of language, and, if we like, further up to an account of the account of language. There is no reason Deleuze should reject this consequence of his thought. Does the language of his view of language burst its own bounds? Of course, and why not?)

VIII

We have seen the traditional view of language as representation and the stabilities that view requires. Deleuze offers a slightly more complex take on the traditional view. For him, it involves three dimensions: denotation, manifestation, and signification. A linguistic claim, a "proposition" as he calls it, operates in these three dimensions. It turns out that these three dimensions require a fourth.

Denotation "is the relation of the proposition to an external state of affairs."[36] It is the proposition's turning outside of itself and pointing toward what it is in the world that it is talking about. The correspondence view of truth is a matter of denotation. When I say "the cow is in the meadow," that proposition refers to the cow, over there, in that particular meadow.

Manifestation "concerns the relation of the proposition to the person who speaks and expresses himself."[37] In manifestation, the proposition also points outside of itself, but this time in another direction. Where denotation points "forward" toward the world the proposition speaks of, manifestation points "backward" toward the proposition's origin, toward the one who utters the proposition.

With denotation and manifestation, we have three intersecting elements in language: a proposition, a speaker, and a state of affairs. These three elements are mutually implicating. Together they form the representational world of language. But if we stop at denotation and manifestation, then we will miss much of what goes on both within language itself and in the relation of language to speaker and world. We need a third concept: signification.

Signification has to do with the implication of propositions, with what follows from a proposition or a group of propositions. It often does not point outside language, but remains within the intralinguistic realm. This can happen in several ways. Deleuze illustrates signification with an example of logical demonstration to show one of them. If two propositions are true, a third one may follow from it. Here is the classic example: 1) All men are mortal; 2) Socrates is a man; 3) Therefore, Socrates is mortal. In this example we don't need to know anything about either denotation or manifestation. It doesn't matter who Socrates is or who is speaking the three propositions. If Socrates were a fictional character and if these sentences were generated by a computer program, the signification would still be the same. The truth of the first two propositions yields the truth of the third one.

Logical demonstrations are not the only kind of signification. Here is another example, still within the intralinguistic realm. There is what is called *material inference*, the direct inference of one proposition from

---

[36] Deleuze, *The Logic of Sense*, p. 12.
[37] Deleuze, *The Logic of Sense*, p. 13.

another. From the proposition "the chair is brown" I can infer immediately another proposition, "the chair is colored." Here there is no
logical demonstration. It is not the combination of two propositions
that yield a third one, but a single proposition that yields another. Like
logical demonstration, though, that yielding is intralinguistic. We do
not infer from the chair's being brown to its being colored by looking
at the chair or by understanding who is talking about the chair. The
inference goes from one linguistic proposition directly to another.

Although much of signification concerns intralinguistic inference,
there can be implications a proposition has that are not intralinguistic.
Deleuze uses the example of a promise. He says that "the assertion of
the conclusion is represented by the moment the promise is kept."[38]
In what way is the keeping of a promise like a logical or material
inference? In what way is keeping a promise like a "conclusion"? If I
offer you a promise, the implication of that offer is that I will fulfill
that promise. The fulfilling of a promise is, in that sense, the "therefore" of the promise. I promise to meet you for coffee at four o'clock.
Therefore, I am committed to be there when I said I would be. It may
turn out that I would like to be somewhere else. Perhaps at half past
three I hear about a radio program I would like to listen to that starts
at four. My promise has implied that I will meet you rather than listen
to the radio program.

Compare that with a logical inference. I am committed to the belief
that all men are mortal and that Socrates is a man. From here, it
does not matter what I would like to believe; I am committed to the
belief that Socrates is mortal. I may deny that Socrates is mortal, just
as I may neglect my meeting with you in order to listen to the radio
program. But in both cases I am rejecting something I am committed
to *by virtue of the language I have used.* In both cases the propositions
have implications: they signify.

Denotation, manifestation, and signification are within the realm
of representation. If they were all there is to language, we would not
escape the dogmatic image of thought. Recall the earlier example
of the cow in the meadow. Denotation would relate the proposition to
the world in a stable way. The words "the cow is in the meadow" would
represent the cow that is out there in the meadow. Manifestation would

[38] Deleuze, *The Logic of Sense*, p. 14.

point back toward a stable speaker that is uttering the words, a person who has processed the image of the cow and can express that image in words. Signification would take us away from the immediate situation involving the cow, the words, and the speaker, but without losing any stability. One implication of the words that were spoken is that there is a mammal in the meadow. There is an inference here, but no loss of stability. Representation remains intact. The move from one part of language to another is just as stable as the move from language to world and language to speaker.

This is a realm in which good sense and common sense reign supreme. There are stable linguistic identities that are coordinated among themselves and in relation to both speaker and world.

This leads to the question: "Is this all there is to language?" For Deleuze, there is more. Alongside the three dimensions of denotation, manifestation, and signification, there is another. "Sense is the fourth dimension of the proposition. The Stoics discovered it along with the event: sense, *the expressed of the proposition*, is an incorporeal, complex, and irreducible entity, at the surface of things, a pure event which inheres or subsists in the proposition."[39] We must ask what this sense is.

IX

We have seen the concept of expression before. Spinoza's substance is expressed in attributes and modes. Likewise, sense is expressed in propositions. But what is this sense?

Sense is what happens at the point at which language and the world meet. It is the happening, the event that arises when a particular proposition comes in contact with the world. This sounds like denotation, but it isn't. Consider this. In denotation, a proposition *refers* to the world it is discussing. If we appeal to the correspondence theory of truth, a true proposition *corresponds* to the world. But what do we mean by *refers* and *corresponds*? We cannot answer this question by turning back to denotation, since that is where the question began. Neither manifestation nor signification will help us either. The question is not one of who is

[39] Deleuze, *The Logic of Sense*, p. 19.

speaking, nor of the implications of a proposition. It is a question of the relation between the proposition and the world.

If we cannot answer this question along these three dimensions, then perhaps there is a fourth one. This is the dimension of sense. "It is exactly the boundary between propositions and things."[40] This boundary is one that eludes capture by the three dimensions of language that constitute its representational structure. That elusiveness should not lead us to dismiss it, however. It is a virtual dimension of language whose reality lies neither in what words nor the world present us with but in what happens when they meet.

A man walks into a bank. He pulls out a gun and says, "This is a stickup." His words denote that the bank is being robbed. They manifest his intention. They signify, among other things, that the man holding the gun is not a security guard. But the words do something else as well. They intersect with the situation in order to create something that was not there before, something that cannot be captured in the traditional view of language, something that overflows it.

Deleuze says that sense is the *expressed* of the proposition and the *attribute* of the state of affairs.[41] We may ask what he is doing when he uses these terms; but we must bear in mind that Deleuze is not representing here. He is palpating.

In his reading of Spinoza, Deleuze emphasizes that when substance is expressed in its attributes and modes, it is absorbed into them. This does not mean that it becomes an attribute or a mode, but that it inheres in them. It does not exist outside them. It is not transcendent. The discussion of science offers us examples of inherence. The constitution of matter allows it, under conditions far from equilibrium, to exhibit the qualities of a chemical clock or bifurcation. This constitution is an aspect of matter that inheres in it and that, under certain conditions, can be expressed. But it cannot be derived from a study of the identity of matter. It is a *differential* aspect of matter. So it is with sense. Sense is expressed in propositions; it inheres in them. But it is not reducible to the qualities of the proposition that expresses it. It is different in kind from the proposition in which it inheres. It is an event that happens in the proposition but is not the proposition itself. The

[40] Deleuze, *The Logic of Sense*, p. 22.
[41] Deleuze, *The Logic of Sense*, pp. 21–2.

words "This is a stickup" do more than any analysis of the meaning of that proposition would be able to tell us.

The other side of sense faces the world; it is the attribute of things or of states of affairs – "although sense does not exist outside of the proposition which expresses it, it is nevertheless the attribute of states of affairs and not the attribute of the proposition. The event subsists in language, but happens to things."[42] A man announces "This is a stickup," and something happens to the world.

How does an event happen to things? For Deleuze, it is by means of verbs, particularly verbs in the infinitive form. "'Green' designates a quality, a mixture of things, a mixture of tree and air where chlorophyll coexists with all parts of the leaf. 'To green,' on the contrary, is not a quality in the thing, but an attribute which is said of the thing."[43]

To green is not to have something happen in the world that changes it from a previous state of affairs into a later one. *To green* does not insert itself into the causal order of things. In that sense, it remains within the proposition. But in another sense, it does happen to things. It happens to them by way of their becoming something through the proposition. When *to green* happens, an aspect of the world is opened up in a new way, something is attributed to it that is beyond the causal order of things. Claire Colebrook, commenting on Deleuze's analysis of sense, puts it this way: "Sense is a power of *incorporeal transformation*: whether I refer to the cut (actual) body as 'injured', 'scarred', or 'punished' will alter what it is in its incorporeal or virtual being. Sense is an event, producing new lines of becoming."[44]

Isn't Deleuze saying something very simple here? Isn't he saying that when we use the word "green" we make the world appear a certain way for the people who hear us? When I say "the leaf is green," aren't I just ascribing a quality to something in the world, manifesting myself in words that denote the world?

That aspect of *green* is what Deleuze is talking about when he says that green designates a quality. He does not deny that this occurs. It occurs in the representational order of things. But he insists that something else occurs as well, something that eludes that representational order

[42] Deleuze, *The Logic of Sense*, p. 24.
[43] Deleuze, *The Logic of Sense*, p. 21.
[44] Colebrook, *Gilles Deleuze*, p. 60.

but is just as real as that order. "The verb has two poles: the present, which indicates its relation to a denotable state of affairs in view of a physical time characterized by succession; and the infinitive, which indicates its relation to sense or the event in view of the internal time which it envelops."[45] To green, to be a stickup, is to orient bodies in certain ways, to create new lines of engagement among things, to cut a trajectory through the world, a trajectory in which both oneself and the world are affected. It is not a matter of representation but of an event that occurs both within and through language, at its point of intersection with the world.

This may sound like Bergson. It should. Bergson also divided time into two types, the time of the succession of moments and the internal time of *durée* or duration. Duration is virtual; it inheres in the time of succession as well as giving rise to it. The infinitive does much the same thing. *To green* does not turn part of the world green. Nor does it point to the already existing greenness of part of the world. It is neither language imposed upon the world nor language reflecting or representing the way the world already is. It is instead a meeting point of the language and the world (but from the side of language, of the proposition), the point at which something happens to both. *To green* indicates both the becoming green of part of the world and the speaking green of language. It is their co-emergence. *The event subsists in language, but it happens to things.*

Sense is the concept Deleuze substitutes for correspondence. In representation, there is supposed to be a match between our words and the world they represent. The difficulty lies in saying what that match is. As we have seen, the match, the correspondence, cannot be accounted for in any of the three dimensions of representational language. Correspondence is what is supposed to explain denotation, and it cannot be explained by means of either manifestation or signification. Deleuze's suggestion is that what happens between propositions and things is either not really or at least not only some kind of match or correspondence. What happens is something that overflows any kind of a correspondence, something that points both toward the world and toward propositions without being reducible to any of the identities of representation or the dogmatic image of the world.

[45] Deleuze, *The Logic of Sense*, p. 184.

Because of this, Deleuze says, sense is paradoxical. We must understand the term *paradoxical* in at least two ways.[46] First, paradox contrasts
with *doxa*. Recall that *doxa* is the common opinion. It is what everyone
knows. "Paradox is opposed to *doxa*, in both aspects of *doxa*, namely,
good sense and common sense."[47] Where *doxa* gives us stable entities
out in the world that correspond to distinct but converging faculties,
paradox points to the unstable character of the relationship of language and world. What happens between language and world is not
simply a tidy match but rather a complex event, an event that only later
gets honed by the dogmatic image of thought into something smooth.

Second, paradox points in two directions at once. It points both
toward the proposition in which it subsists and toward the world of
which it is an attribute. But this pointing in two directions at once is
not like a double arrow that can point at once to the east and to the
west. The east and the west are both directions in space. They are of
the same kind, the same category. To point to the east is simply the
opposite of pointing to the west.

Language and world are not symmetrical like that. It is only representation, which would like to have a concept of correspondence,
that wants to find the moment of symmetry between the two. Paradox points in two directions at once, but the things it points to are
of a divergent nature. One cannot take the arrow of sense, remove
it from a proposition, place it in the world, and then point back toward language. Paradox involves the bringing together of disparate
elements into a convergence that neither reduces one to the other
nor keeps them apart. This asymmetry between language and world
points toward something deeper than sense, something Deleuze calls
nonsense.

X

To grasp what Deleuze is palpating with the concept of *nonsense*, we
must first understand something about the structuralist theory of language developed by the Swiss linguist Ferdinand de Saussure. The

---

[46] There are, in fact, other paradoxes. Deleuze discusses them in *The Logic of Sense*,
especially pp. 28–35 and pp. 74–81.
[47] Deleuze, *The Logic of Sense*, p. 75.

book developed from Saussure's lectures, translated into English as
Course in General Linguistics,[48] is undoubtedly the linguistic text that
has most influenced twentieth-century French philosophy. The anthropological structuralism of Claude Lévi-Strauss, the psychoanalysis
of Jacques Lacan, the Marxism of Louis Althusser, and Derrida's deconstruction all owe deep debts to Saussure. In *The Logic of Sense*, Deleuze
does not discuss Saussure's linguistics in depth.[49] However, Saussure's
linguistics are there in the background, as they are for every French
thinker of Deleuze's generation.

Saussure sees the structure of language, both in its meaning and
in its phonetics, as a matter of differences rather than elements: "in
language there are only differences *without positive terms.*"[50] Phonetics
provides the most straightforward example. Suppose I want to pro-
nounce the sound corresponding to the letter *b*. We can call it the
b-sound. There is no exact sound I have to make. What gives the phonetic quality to the b-sound is not the sound itself but its difference
from surrounding similar sounds, for example d-sounds and t-sounds.
It is the contrast between sounds rather than the sounds themselves
that give the phonemes their particular phonetic place in language.

If it were the positive terms – the sounds themselves – rather than the
differences among them that gave sounds their phonetic place, then
we would never be able to understand people with different accents
or different ways of speaking. This is because people with different
accents speak sounds differently. (This is often especially true with
vowels.) In fact, each person speaks sounds slightly differently. So if
there had to be an exact sound corresponding to, say, the b-sound, almost nobody would understand it. Instead, a range of different sounds
can fall under the category of the b-sound. What limits that range is the
range of other letters that contrast with it, like t-sounds and d-sounds.

This differential system also applies to the meanings of words. The
meaning of the word *tree* is neither a specific concept in my head nor
any particular tree out there, but the role of the term in the language,
particularly in contrast to other terms such as *bush, shrub, plant,* and so

---

[48] The lectures from which this book is drawn were given between 1906 and 1911.
[49] In his later collaboration with Guattari, Deleuze often borrows concepts from the
work of structuralist Hjelmslev, a disciple of Saussure.
[50] Saussure, *Course in General Linguistics*, p. 120.

on. If there were no words like these in English, the word *tree* would
have a different role to play. Thus, as Saussure says, the meaning of a
term in a language is defined by its role in that language, and its role
is defined by the differences between it and other terms.

If we now relate language to the world, we have a complex situation
involving two groups (or what Deleuze calls *series*) of differences. On
the one hand, being is difference. The world arises from the actualization of a virtual difference that underlies and inhabits that actualization. The science of Monod and Prigogine, as well as the reflections
of Bergson and Nietzsche, have taught us this. On the other hand
language is a system of differences. It exists not as a system of positive elements, each of which has its identity. Rather it is defined by
differences that, like the difference of being, can be palpated but not
brought under representational categories. To speak, then, is to bring
two series of differences into contact: being and language.

For Deleuze, this contact between two series of differences implies
the existence of certain kinds of paradoxical elements that belong
to both and neither series at the same time. "The two heterogeneous series converge toward a paradoxical element, which is their
'differentiator'. . . . This element belongs to no series; or rather, it belongs to both series at once and never ceases to circulate among
them."[51] This paradoxical element, the element that both is and is
not of language, and is and is not of the world, is nonsense.

The role of nonsense is "to traverse the heterogeneous series, to
make them resonate and converge, but also to ramify them and to
introduce into each one of them multiple disjunctions. It is word = x
and thing = x."[52] In order to see what this role is, Deleuze often
appeals to Lewis Carroll. Here is an exchange between Alice and the
Red Knight from *Through the Looking Glass:*

"The name of the song is called '*Haddocks' Eyes.*'"
"Oh, that's the name of the song, is it?" Alice said, trying to feel interested.
"No, you don't understand," the Knight said, looking a little vexed. "That's
what the name of the song is *called.* The name is really '*The Aged Aged Man*'."
"Then I ought to have said, "That's what the *song* is called?" Alice corrected
herself.

[51] Deleuze, *The Logic of Sense*, pp. 50–1.
[52] Deleuze, *The Logic of Sense*, p. 66.

"No, you oughtn't: that's quite another thing! The *song* is called '*Ways And Means*': but that's only what it's *called*, you know!"

"Well, what *is* the song, then?" said Alice, who by this time was completely bewildered."[53]

Here, of course, the Red Knight sings the song. Because that is what the song *is*.

In this exchange, the movement goes from what the name of the song is called to what the name of the song is, to what the song itself is called, to what the song is. In this shift, the idea of a name begins to do double-duty. It is both language and world, in the sense that it is what does the referring and what is referred to.[54] It is both language and the object of language. In this case, of course, what does the referring and what is referred to are both a single piece of language, a name. And that is where nonsense arises. Nonsense is a paradoxical element that, in this case, "ramifies" the series from what the name of the song is called to the name of the song, and so on.

Lewis Carroll's writings proliferate these forms of nonsense. This proliferation is not, for Deleuze, merely a game that can be played at the margins of language. It points to something essential about language itself. It is nonsense that allows language and the world to come together. It is only because there can be these paradoxical elements that both bring language and world together and keep them separate that there can be linguistic meaning at all. Without this paradox, there would only be the non-communication of these two series, a silence between them.

The realm of difference that is the world and the realm of difference that is language are brought together and kept apart by nonsense, a paradoxical element that "traverses" them. Deleuze sometimes calls this paradoxical element, this nonsense, the "empty square." Moreover, it is only on the basis of nonsense that sense can arise.

Authors referred to as "structuralists" by recent practice may have no essential point in common other than this: sense, regarded not at all as appearance but

---

[53] Carroll, *The Annotated Alice*, p. 306.

[54] There is complication here. For Saussure, the distinction between signifier and signified is a distinction between the language that does the referring and the *concept* it refers to. The signified is a concept, not the world itself. Deleuze does not always follow this usage, since for him the heterogeneous series that resonate through nonsense can just as easily be world and language as concepts and language.

as surface effect and position effect, and produced by the circulation of the empty square in the structural series...structuralism shows in this manner that sense is produced by nonsense and its perpetual displacement, and that it is born of the respective position of elements which are not in themselves "signifying."[55]

What, then, is the relation between sense and nonsense? Sense is the paradoxical element that resides in the proposition but is the attribute of things. Nonsense is the paradoxical element that circulates among language and things and brings them together. Sense is "exactly the boundary between propositions and things." But is that not what nonsense is? And if so, what is the difference between them?

Sense is produced by nonsense. To grasp this thought, we need to bear in mind that nonsense is not a *something*. If it is an element, as Deleuze sometimes calls it, it is an element that is not a particular thing but a paradox. What gives the nonsensical character to the passage on names from *Through the Looking Glass* is that the names both are and are not from the series of language. They are both signifying and signified. It is from the movement of this paradox that sense arises, not as a thing emerging from another thing, but as an effect of the movement itself. "In short, sense is always an *effect*. It is not an effect merely in the causal sense; it is also an effect in the sense of an 'optical effect' or a 'sound effect,' or, even better, a surface effect, a position effect, and a language effect."[56]

It is because there is nonsense, because something can bring together the series that is being (or the world) and the series that is language and circulate between and among them, that there can be sense. Sense is an effect of nonsense: it is caused by this bringing together and it arises on its surface. It is like a sound effect or an optical effect because it is not produced by nonsense in any traditional causal sense. It is not like the sound that is produced when a bat hits a ball. Sense is incorporeal; it is not inserted into the causal order of material things. Optical effects and sound effects happen when a certain way of being seen or being heard emerges from an optical or sonic arrangement. What are called optical illusions are like this. Draw a certain pattern

---

55 Deleuze, *The Logic of Sense*, p. 71.
56 Deleuze, *The Logic of Sense*, p. 70.

on paper and the eyes see something more than is drawn. This doesn't just have to do with the lines on the paper, nor with the eyes, but with what happens between them, with what Deleuze might call a certain nonsense that circulates in their interaction.

So it is with sense. Nonsense circulates between and among the differences of language and the world. In that circulation, language and the world offer certain ways of being "proposed." A "proposition," which is what has a sense, is a way of their being proposed. It is both an effect of that circulation and a proposal within language for the world.

XI

I say, "The leaf is green." That is a proposition. There is sense to this proposition. It lies in the *to green* of the leaf. The *to green* inheres in the proposition, but it is attributed to the world. The *to green* is not denotation, not manifestation, not signification. It is that which gives rise to the denotation in "The leaf is green"; it remains virtually in that denotation; but it cannot itself be denoted.

How can there be sense? How can a proposition have sense? It can do so because the series of differences that is the world and the series of differences that is language can be brought together by a paradoxical element that makes them both converge and diverge. Sense happens on the basis of this convergence and divergence. And sense, in turn, stirs our words beyond – and within – their denotation, their manifestation, and their signification, making something happen to us and to the world. Just as the world is not inert, is not merely a matter of identities, so language is not inert, not merely a matter of representation.

Language is always more than language. Or better, language is always more than representation. It spills over into the world. It is woven into the world in order to be able to function as representation. This weaving requires paradoxes, paradoxes of sense and nonsense that escape the grasp of language. "It is language which fixes the limits (the moment, for example, at which the excess begins), but it is language as well which transcends the limits and restores them to the infinite equivalence of an unlimited becoming."[57]

---

[57] Deleuze, *The Logic of Sense*, pp. 2–3.

To affirm language, then, is to affirm becoming. It is to palpate that in language which is beyond representation. It is to recognize the paradoxical elements that are its virtual character, and that always exist in any act of representation. Whatever we see, whatever we say, there is more, always more.

XII

To learn is to enter into the universal of the relations which constitute the Idea, and into their corresponding singularities. The idea of the sea, for example, as Leibniz showed, is a system of liaisons or differential relations between particulars and singularities corresponding to the degrees of variation among these relations – the totality of the system being incarnated in the real movement of the waves. To learn to swim is to conjugate the distinctive points of our bodies with the singular points of the objective Idea in order to form a problematic field.[58]

What does learning consist in? Here is a traditional view: learning is a matter of memorizing something that somebody else knows. It sounds simplistic, if we put it that way. But who among us has not attended high school and college and has not been subjected to this view of learning? A teacher, a professor, stands before the class, chalk or transparencies in hand. There are *things* you need to learn, *items* you need to know. Before the class period is over, these things will be transferred from the teacher's lecture notes, the professor's transparencies, to your notebook. From there, these things will be transferred to your brain. When these transfers are successful, you will be said to have learned what the teacher, the professor, has to teach you.

It is a meager model of learning. It is also the most common one. It is a model that operates on some surface assumptions and a slightly deeper one. Its surface assumptions are, first, that the teacher knows what there is to know about a subject and you do not. Second, there is the assumption that the way that you learn what the teacher knows is to listen to the teacher and commit to memory what he or she has to say. Last, on the teacher's side, there is the assumption that by talking or using other media to substitute for talking, the teacher can impart to the student what needs to be known.

---

[58] Deleuze, *Difference and Repetition*, p. 165.

The slightly deeper assumption has to do with the dogmatic image of thought. It is the assumption that what is to be learned comes in discrete packets of identities. There are particular *somethings* that need to be known. These somethings may be related to one another or they may not. In either case, they are independent enough from one another to be isolated each to a sentence, a paragraph, or a chapter. These somethings are then represented by the sentences spoken by the teacher or professor, and then arrive in your ear or on your paper. If the learning is successful, there will have been no alteration, no damage, of any of these somethings along the way. Their identities will retain their integrity. And if you do your job you will be able to repeat or manipulate these identities when test time comes around.

There is another view of learning that does not start with the assumption that what is to be learned has the character of an identity or group of identities. It starts instead from the assumption that what there is to be learned has the character of difference rather than identity. If what is to be learned does not have the character of identity, then the learning itself is not a project of transferring identities from the knower to the one who seeks to know. It is instead a project of experimentation.

Swimmers do not learn facts about the water and about their bodies and then apply them to the case at hand. The water and their bodies are swarms of differences. In order to navigate their bodies through the water they will need to acquire a skill: to "conjugate" their bodies with the water in such a way as to stay on its surface. This skill involves no memorization. It involves an immersion, a finding one's way through things, coming through one's body to understand what one is capable of in the water. There is no one way to do this, and different ways may lead to different kinds of success. There are also failures; water may be composed of differences, but not every path through those differences will keep one afloat.

Swimmers apprentice themselves to the water. They get a feel for the water, for how it moves and what possibilities it offers them. They get a feel for their bodies in the water. And they conjugate one against the other. The couplet body/water is a problematic field, in the sense of the word *problem* we saw earlier. Particular ways of swimming are solutions within that problematic field. They do not solve *the* problem of swimming. For there is no single problem of swimming.

There is instead a problematic field of body/water, of which particular ways of swimming are solutions. They are experiments in conjugation of this problematic field, much of which takes place below the level of conscious thought, beneath the identities representation offers to us: "'learning' always takes place in and through the unconscious, thereby establishing a profound complicity between nature and mind."[59]

What does learning how to *think* consist in? Unlike learning how to swim, it first requires the abandonment of bad habits. These habits are the ones instilled in all of us by the dogmatic image of thought and its representational view of language and the world. We must discover this image and this view; we must see what roles they play in preventing us from really thinking.

But that is not all. That is only the negative task, the clearing of the ground. Alongside this abandonment we must also experiment in ways of thinking. We must conjugate our thought and our world, our thought and our language.

There are those who have gone before us, who have swum in this water before: Spinoza, Bergson, Nietzsche among them. They may help ease us into the water, teach us some of the strokes, so we don't drown before we get started. We can apprentice ourselves to them. Sooner or later, however, we must push off from the shore and conjugate things for ourselves. That is what Deleuze does in *Difference and Repetition* and *The Logic of Sense*. But we must all do it for ourselves, each of us. We can apprentice ourselves to Deleuze if we like, as he does with those who come before him. But he cannot swim for us.

There are two mistakes we might make in considering the prospect of learning to think. The first mistake would be to assume that thinking, unlike swimming, is a purely conscious activity, that thinking is a manipulation of thought. That mistake is our inheritance from the dogmatic image of thought. We feel our way into thinking in much the same way as we feel our way into swimming. Thinking is at least as unconscious as it is conscious, and it is no less an experiment. That is one of the things meant by the suggestion that Deleuze *palpates* his subject matter. The second mistake would be to assume that each of us must face this task alone. In fact we can face it in groups, conjugating

---

59 Deleuze, *Difference and Repetition*, p. 165.

ourselves with one another as well as with the world. Thinking does not need to be a solitary activity, and it surely does not take place in a world we do not share with others. The next step, then, might be to consider our place among others in the world, to *think* about it, or with it, or in it.

That step would lead us into politics.

4

The Politics of Difference

I

Here is a way of seeing the world: it is composed not of identities
that form and reform themselves, but of swarms of difference that
actualize themselves into specific forms of identity. Those swarms are
not outside the world; they are not transcendent creators. They are
of the world, as material as the identities formed from them. And
they continue to exist even within the identities they form, not as
identities but as difference. From their place within identities, these
swarms of difference assure that the future will be open to novelty, to
new identities and new relationships among them.

We have seen this world in the thought of Spinoza, Bergson, and
Nietzsche. Spinoza lays the groundwork for thinking the immanence
of difference. Difference is not transcendent creation; it is immanent
expression. Bergson offers the temporal scaffolding for this expression. Time is not a linear passage of discrete instantaneous units but
the actualization of the virtual. Nietzsche announces difference and its
eternal return. He points the way toward affirming the play of chance,
the embrace of the dice throw. He does not regret the openness of the
future, does not reach helplessly toward the security of what he thinks
he knows.

We have seen this world in science and in language. It is the chaos
within physics and biology. It is in the way language overspills itself, always doing more than it can say. And we have begun to think this world

as well, moving beyond the dogmatic image of thought we have inherited toward a new, more agile, thought that palpates what it cannot conceive and gestures at what it cannot grasp.

Is this world one of complete arbitrariness? Can we say nothing of the future on the basis of what is or what has been? Is everything and anything equally possible at every moment?

It is more accurate to say that we do not know what is possible at every moment than to say that everything is possible. To say that everything is possible would be to deny that the world is composed of difference. It would be more like saying the world is *undifferentiated.* If everything were equally possible at every moment, that would be because everything is always there, vying for expression, all the time. That is not what Deleuze says. The world is composed of fields of difference, problematic fields, not fields of undifferentiation. To say that the world is more than we experience is not to say that the world is everything, all the time. To say, with Monod, that "a *totally* blind process can by definition lead to anything; it can even lead to vision itself," is not to say that vision is possible in every biological being at every moment.

Although the future is an actualization of difference, this actualization is constrained by the structure of a particular virtuality. (This was discussed in Chapter 3.) Chemical processes are composed of particular relationships of difference, not of all the differences of being at one time. Moreover, Prigogine's work shows us that the differences inhabiting material forms can only display themselves under certain conditions. A chemical clock cannot occur in conditions that are close to equilibrium, only in conditions that are far from it. The differential relationships that determine chemical processes include both chemical and physical conditions.

The same holds for language. A particular language cannot express all possible forms of sense. (That is why translation can be so difficult.) It can only express what the differential relationships in that language, in their articulation against and across the world, permits.

We might put the point this way: history is not irrelevant. History is the folding and unfolding of particular swarms of difference in particular relationships. It is the virtual character of the past as it inhabits the present. To deny the relevance of history is not simply to deny the identities on which historical study often relies; it is, equally, to deny the realm of difference that inhabits our present.

Perhaps, rather than saying that *anything can happen*, it would be more accurate to say that *anything can happen, given the right conditions*. But, since we do not know of what a body is capable, it would be better to say, not that *anything* can happen, but that *so much* can happen that we do not know about. The world's possibilities are beyond us. We are constrained in opening ourselves to them, not only by the limits of our imagination and the vastness of our ignorance but – and this is what Deleuze means to cure – by the very way we think about those possibilities.

Does this mean that prediction is futile? No. Chemical processes can often be predicted in conditions that are near equilibrium. We can predict the future with some degree of accuracy, the more so if prediction occurs by means of *probabilities* rather than *scientific laws*. The world is a world of difference, not of undifferentiation. And, if we are to live like Nietzsche's bad player, we might seek to reduce the world to its predictability, to take probabilities on the throw of the dice. We would always be impoverished, but not always mistaken, to do so.

But to think about the world's possibilities in a fresh way, to take account of the differences in which we and the world are steeped, requires a new ontology. And so, against the grain carved by Sartre and Derrida and Foucault, Deleuze traces a new ontology, a new way of conceiving of being, the world, or what there is. He takes up the challenge of the limits of our thought in order to construct a new thought. Instead of abandoning the questions of being that have been badly posed by so many of our philosophical ancestors, he chooses to raise them again, but to pose them differently. Being is not a puzzle to be solved but a problem to be engaged. It is to be engaged by a thought that moves as comfortably among problems as it does among solutions, as fluidly among differences as it does among identities.

The task of such thought is not to be undertaken alone. A philosopher in his study understanding the world as difference is not the goal of Deleuze's ontology. The world as Deleuze conceives it is a living world, a vital world. This is true even of the world's inanimate realms. But it is not only a living world; it is a world *to be lived in*. The task is not merely to think the world differently, but to live it differently. As was said at the outset, Deleuze's guide to living is both a guide to conceiving the world as living and a guide to raising the question of how one might live.

And one does not live alone. One lives among others: thinking among them, acting among them, speaking with and struggling among them. For Deleuze's thought to take the next step is for it to start thinking not only the world but the *among others* in which thought takes place. The challenge facing the thought of difference is not only to think the vital difference that is the unfolding of being but also to think the political world in which that thought takes place.

Although Deleuze's earlier works gesture in the direction of politics, it is only when he starts collaborating with Félix Guattari that the thought of difference turns from a general to a political ontology. In Deleuze's own intellectual itinerary, it is after the events of May 1968 in France that politics moves toward the forefront of his thought.[1]

II

Let us start with traditional liberal political theory. (The term *liberal* here is not contrasted with conservative. It is contrasted with sovereign, in the sense of royalty. Both contemporary liberals and conservatives in the United States find their roots in liberal political theory.) Liberal theory is our political inheritance. It is the ether in which debates about the role of the state, the right to abortion, the obligations to immigrants, the reform of welfare, and most other debates in what is called the "public" realm are discussed. Liberal theory authorizes the terms and sets the limits of those debates. For most of us, the framework of liberal theory appears so natural as to be inescapable. How else might we discuss matters of politics?

The starting point for liberal politics is the individual. Earlier political theory starts with the sovereign: the king, the prince, in any case the head of state. The sovereign is the given of early political theory;

---

[1] In May and June 1968, people from very different quarters of life – students, workers, women – took to the streets of Paris, built barricades, defied the police, and almost forced the resignation of then President Charles DeGaulle. He was restored to power with the assistance of the French Communist Party, which resented the fact that the uprising was not being led or controlled by them. In the wake of what came to be called "May '68," French intellectuals began to theorize progressive politics outside the Marxist tradition.

it is the point around which theorizing revolves. Liberal theory reverses the terms of this relation. For liberal theory, it is the individual to be governed, not the governor, who is the starting point. A proper understanding of the political begins with individuals and their relationship to one another, not with an already constituted state and its royal prerogatives.

The founding question for liberal theory is: "Why should an individual consent to be governed in the first place?" This is the question posed by the initiators of the liberal tradition, thinkers like Thomas Hobbes, John Locke, and Thomas Jefferson. It remains the question for contemporary political theory. John Rawls and Robert Nozick have not shifted the question. They, and others whose writings trace the parameters of our political thought, remain bound to the same starting point. There are individual human beings, each with his or her interests, goals, and particular characteristics. Why and under what conditions should these individuals come together and allow themselves to be governed?

The various answers offered to this question constitute the substance of the liberal political tradition. That variance is a product of different assumptions about the needs of individuals, their willingness to cooperate with one another, their motivation to abide by rules to which they have agreed, the dangers of consolidating political power, the likelihood and depth of conflicts between the better off and the worse off, and the range of individual liberty that is the birthright of individuals.

People in America who call themselves *liberals* (in the everyday sense of the term) make certain assumptions, or argue for certain positions, on these matters. People who call themselves *conservatives* arrange their assumptions differently. Liberals, for instance, are wont to weigh heavily the needs of individuals, to count on people's willingness to cooperate with one another, and to be more willing to limit certain individual liberties for the collective good. Conservatives are more likely to be concerned about the dangers of consolidating political power, more enthusiastic about individual liberties, and less concerned about conflicts between the better off and the worse off. What both groups agree on is that these matters are the proper ones to be discussed, and that their discussion is ultimately addressed to the question of why individuals should allow themselves to be governed.

What does government do, then? What is its role? In some form or another, it *represents* individuals and their interests. If a government is to be a legitimate one, the interests of each individual must be represented in the public realm occupied by government. I can only be asked to consent to be governed if the structure of government takes the realization of my interests as its task and its goal. This does not mean that a government must attempt to realize all of my interests. People have different and conflicting interests; not all of them can be realized. However, for a government to be legitimate is for it to recognize those interests and to attempt to arrange the cooperative aspects of our lives in such a way as to meet the most important of them, and to allow us to pursue them as best we can.

This is what has come to be known as the social contract. Each individual, deciding on his or her own, agrees to come together under a common government, and agrees to obey that government, as long as the government the individual agrees to obey is one that represents his or her most important interests.

A government that does not start from the interests of the governed, that does not represent those interests, has lost its mandate to govern. This need not be a serious matter. If the problem lies with the particular participants in the governing body, then they can be removed by the individuals they govern. In the standard case, they are voted out of office. By contrast, if the problem is deeper, if the government is not structured in such a way as to represent the interests of the governed, then those individuals are justified in forming a new, more representative, governmental structure. The early slogan of the American Revolution, "no taxation without representation," is an example of this. The colonials' complaint was not that the particular members of Parliament did not have their interests in mind when deciding tax policy; it was that the British government was structured to prevent any of the colonials from having their interests represented. To address that problem required a new, more representative, form of government.

This picture of politics constitutes the framework within which we discuss political issues. It is the element of our political thought. No doubt it is an advance on sovereign political theory. Better to see things from the side of the governed than from the side of the governor. But neither is there any doubt that liberal political theory is a form of the dogmatic image of thought. It is precisely the dogmatic image translated into political terms.

For the dogmatic image of thought, there are already constituted identities, each with its qualities, which are to be represented by thought. For liberal political theory, there are already constituted individuals, each with his or her interests (although these interests are usually seen as chosen rather than already attached to the individual), which are to be represented by government. For the dogmatic image of thought, representation is the relay from the world to thought. For liberal political theory, representation is the relay from the individual to government. For the dogmatic image of thought, truth consists in the correspondence between thought and the identities it represents. For liberal political theory, legitimacy or justice consists in the correspondence between government and the individuals it represents.

Identities and representation: this is the stuff of the dogmatic image of thought. It is mirrored precisely in liberal political theory. No wonder stability is a constant preoccupation of political discussion. No wonder the threat to politics is so often called *anarchy*, by which is meant chaos, by which is meant instability and disorder. Politics is a matter of stability, of the stable representation of given individual interests by means of a government that considers and balances those interests in the public realm.

There are many questions that have been posed to liberal political theory, particularly in recent years. Does it make sense to conceive individuals as choosing their specific interests; doesn't the society one is brought up in and lives in contribute to the character of those interests? In populous societies, how is government to represent individuals' interests; what are the proper regional or geographic parameters for governments? How should we conceive representation; to what degree is an elected representative obliged to speak in the name of those represented when their views on a particular issue diverge from his or hers? Most of these questions share important elements of traditional liberal theory. They are attempts to modify rather than to eliminate the framework for liberal thought.

The question for Deleuze, the political question, is whether we can think otherwise. Is politics necessarily hostage to the dogmatic image of thought, or can we think about politics differently? Can we live together differently? Is there more to our political lives than has been accounted for by the dogmatic image embraced by the liberal tradition?

III

One way to approach Deleuze and Guattari's politics is to see them as offering a new political ontology. Deleuze cannot accept the dogmatic ontology offered by traditional political theory. To begin our political thought with individual human beings, each of which comes with his or her own (chosen) interests, is already to give the game away. It is to concede the stability of the already given that is the foundation of the dogmatic image of thought.

The problem is not only that individuals' interests are intimately bound up with the society in which they live. It is true, as the communitarians[2] have pointed out, that liberal political theory's isolation of individuals from their societies often paints a distorted view of people's interests. Individuals are far more subject to their social surroundings than liberal theory would have us believe. But the problem Deleuze sees is deeper. It lies in the very concept of the individual.

Why should we assume that individual human beings are the proper ontological units for political theory? Is it possible to start with some other unit? Or better, is it possible to start with a concept that is not prejudiced toward any particular unit of political analysis, whether it be the individual, the society, the state, the ethnic group, or whatever? Is it possible to conceive politics on the basis of a more fluid ontology, one that would allow for political change and experimentation on a variety of levels, rather than privileging one level or another?

In the collaborative work Deleuze and Guattari perform together, they offer a variety of starting places, a variety of concepts that are agile enough to insert at different political levels. One of the concepts they rely on the most is that of the *machine*. "Everywhere *it* [what Freud called the id] is machines – real ones, not figurative ones: machines driving other machines, machines being driven by other machines, with all the necessary couplings and connections. . . . we are all

---

[2] For example, Michael Sandel in his book *Liberalism and the Limits of Justice.*

handymen: each with his little machines."[3] The machine is a concept that can be situated at the level of the individual, the society, the state, the pre-individual, among groups and between people, and across these various realms. It is a concept that offers ontological mobility, and thus can capture what overspills the dogmatic image of political thought.

Claire Colebrook offers a suggestive contrast. She writes that:

> In *Anti-Oedipus* and *A Thousand Plateaus* Deleuze and Guattari use a terminology of machines, assemblages, connections and productions. . . . An *organism* is a bounded whole with an identity and an end. A *mechanism* is a closed machine with a specific function. A *machine*, however, is nothing more than its connections; it is not made by anything, is not for anything, and has no closed identity."[4]

An organism is a self-regulating whole. Each of its parts supports others, and the whole is the harmony of those parts. We often conceive biological entities as organisms in this sense, and the wonder we feel at them comes from the balance of their living elements. If biologists like Simondon and Monod are right, however, there are no such things as organisms, at least in this sense. It is not that there is no balance among various organic parts. Often there is. It is that there is always more to the parts than their balance, a *more* that can express itself in other directions, with other balances, or with no balance at all.

This does not mean only that there can be a different balance among the same parts. It means, first, that there can be a different individual. We saw the argument by Barry Commoner that genetic engineering can result in very different biological forms from the ones engineers might predict. Beyond that, there can be different relations with different parts of the environment. A different biological entity may interact with different aspects or elements of the environment. It may eat different things; it may nest in different places; it may dig up different parts of the earth; it may clear different paths; ultimately, it may be eaten by different biological entities.

One way to capture this point would be to say that we should think of biological entities not as self-sustaining organisms but as mobile

---

[3] Deleuze and Guattari, *Anti-Oedipus: Capitalism and Schizophrenia*, p. 1.
[4] Colebrook, *Gilles Deleuze*, p. 56.

machines that may connect to the environment in a variety of ways, depending on how those machines are actualized.

If machines are not organisms, neither are they mechanisms. Mechanisms are machines in their frozen state. They are machines caught at a particular moment in time, in the seeming solidity of particular connections. Mechanisms are machines seen from the viewpoint of the present instant, machines seen spatially in Bergson's sense. Mechanisms are the actualization of machines. Our perception may encounter mechanisms; but our thought must penetrate those mechanisms in order to discover the machines within them.

Colebrook offers this example. "Think of a bicycle, which obviously has no 'end' or intention. It only works when it is connected with another 'machine' such as the human body. . . . But we could imagine different connections producing different machines. The cycle becomes an art object when placed in a gallery; the human body becomes an 'artist' when connected with a paintbrush."[5] Here there are seven machines: the bicycle, the human body, the gallery, the paintbrush, the bicycle-body, the bicycle-gallery, the body-paintbrush. Let us take two of these. The bicycle is composed of a series of connections among its parts (each of which are, in turn, composed of a series of connections among their molecular parts). It is their connections that create the machine that is a bicycle. The bicycle-body is another machine, formed from another set of connections: foot-to-pedal, hand-to-handlebar, rear-end-to-seat.

If we think this way, then the concept of a machine becomes agile. It applies not only to bicycles, but also to parts of bicycles and to things of which bicycles are themselves parts. There is no privileged unit of analysis. We will go on to apply this concept to politics. But even now, before we do that, we can see one of its virtues. Liberal political theory's reliance on the concept of the individual as the pivot of political analysis forces it to approach politics mechanistically or organically. The relation of individuals to society is one of a specific set of connections or a self-organizing whole. To think machinically is to consider the relation of individuals to society as only one level of connections that can be discussed. One can also discuss pre-individual connections and supra-individual connections.

---

5 Colebrook, *Gilles Deleuze*, p. 56.

Moreover, these connections can be seen in their fluidity. Individuals, in the liberal tradition, are pre-given. They come with their (chosen) interests, wearing them like sandwich boards. "I am Bob. My interests are: skateboarding, eating Chinese food, reading cyberpunk fiction." But individuals have changing interests that emerge from their changing connections to their changing environments. Machinic thinking recognizes these changes. Machines are not mechanisms; they evolve, mutate, and reconnect with different machines, which are themselves in evolution and mutation.

A third point. Machinic connections are productive. They are creative. Deleuze and Guattari emphasize this point in *Anti-Oedipus* as a contrast to psychoanalytic thinking. For psychoanalysis, desire is conceived in terms of lack. I desire what I want but do not have. If we think of desire machinically, however, it loses its character of lack. Desire is a creator of connections, not a lack that must be filled. To desire is to connect with others: sexually, politically, athletically, gastronomically, vocationally. "The breast is a machine that produces milk, and the mouth a machine coupled to it. The mouth of an anorexic wavers between several functions: its possessor is uncertain as to whether it is an eating-machine, an anal machine, a talking-machine, or a breathing machine (asthma attacks)."[6] Machines do not fill lacks; they connect, and through connecting create.

Deleuze and Guattari's critique of psychoanalysis has bearing on liberal political theory. Liberal theory thinks of individuals in terms of what they lack politically. It is not that the individuals are constituted by any internal lacks of the kind psychoanalysis claims. There is no missing mother figure that an individual's desire is forever chasing. The individual is a whole; the individual has chosen his or her own interests. Nothing is lacking in that sense. But individuals are unable to realize their interests on their own. There is a lack, not within them, but between their interests and the environment in which they pursues them. The environment does not immediately provide the resources to realize their interests. If there were no lack in this sense, there would be no motivation to consent to be governed.

The answer to the question of why individuals would allow themselves to be governed always concerns their inability to fulfill their

---

[6] Deleuze and Guattari, *Anti-Oedipus*, p. 1.

interests on their own. That inability could be due to scarcity, to competition from others, or to the complexity of the interests themselves. But for one reason or another, individuals need others in order to satisfy their desires or realize their interests. The idea of lack is central to liberal political theory. It motivates the social contract. It is what binds the fates of individuals to the fates of other individuals.

Machines do not operate out of lack. They do not seek to fulfill needs. Instead they produce connections. Moreover, the connections they produce are not pre-given; machines are not mechanisms. Machines are productive in unpredictable and often novel ways.

The concept of a machine as Deleuze and Guattari employ it is like the concept of difference Deleuze develops before his collaboration with Guattari. If the individual is the central political concept of the dogmatic image of thought, then the machine can stand as a central political concept of the new form of thought Deleuze develops. It imports into politics three characteristics of Deleuze's general ontology.

First, machines retain Deleuze's concept of difference as positive rather than negative. Recall his critique of traditional concepts of difference. Difference is subordinated to identity; difference is what is *not* identical. This is difference seen as lack: difference is the lack of identity, the privation of sameness. But difference does not have to be cast in the role of lack or negativity. The appeal of the concept of difference to Deleuze is that if one can conceive it positively rather than negatively, it shows that there is more to the world than meets the eye. That is how machines function. In their distinction from mechanisms, machines are mobile producers of connections. They are not reducible to any one set of connections, any particular identity. Even when they are connected in a particular way they are capable of other connections and other functions. We can call this the Nietzschean character of machines.

How are they capable of this mobility? It is because machines are not reducible to their actual connections. There is a virtuality to machines that inheres in any set of actual connections and that allows them to connect in other and often novel ways. Bicycles are means of transportation, art objects, sources of spare parts, items in an exchange economy, objects of childhood fantasy – all depending on what other machines they connect to. We can call this the Bergsonian character of machines.

Finally, the virtual character of machines, their mobility as machines
and the mobility of the concept *machine*, does not come from their
transcendent character. It is not because machines stand outside their
connections that they are capable of such mobility. There is no such
thing as a machine outside of its connections. It is within their connections, and perhaps sometimes through them, that machines are
capable of producing other connections. The root of a tree can connect through the soil to the foundation of a house, where it produces
a crack that allows moles to burrow through. Deleuze and Guattari
call the schizoanalysis they develop in *Anti-Oedipus* a materialist psychiatry, in contrast to the transcendent psychiatry of psychoanalysis. A
materialist psychiatry does not see a transcendent figure (for example,
Oedipus) organizing the connections that are made. The connections
arise from within matter; they are not imposed from the outside. We
can call this the Spinozist character of machines.

"We define social formations by *machinic processes* and not by modes
of production (these on the contrary depend on the processes)."[7]
In contrast to Freud, there is no organizing element to "desiring-
machines" that imposes specific modes of connections from outside
or above. In contrast to Marx, economic modes of production do not
define machinic connections. Rather, it is the other way around: economic modes of production are defined by the character of their machinic connections. The *machine* is a concept that can be developed to
form a Deleuzian political ontology that avoids the dogmatic image of
thought that structures liberal political theory.

IV

To embrace the concept of the machine is to move from a focus on the
macropolitical to the micropolitical, from the molar to the molecular.
The distinction between these two pairs of terms is one of the most
misunderstood in Deleuze's thought. It is only when the concept of
the machine is grasped that we begin to understand the role they are
meant to play.

The misunderstanding of macropolitical and micropolitical, or molar and molecular, goes like this. The macropolitical concerns large

[7] Deleuze and Guattari, *A Thousand Plateaus*, p. 435.

political entities or institutions or historical forces. Liberals who focus on the state and Marxists who focus on the economy are macropolitical theorists. They overlook the small elements that comprise our political lives. They are fascinated by the grand scheme of things. In order to understand how we are constructed and how power works, however, we must turn from the grand scale to the smaller scale. We must focus on the little things. We must exchange the telescope for the microscope. Only then will we see the political power at work.

This is a good schema for grasping the thought of Foucault. He analyzes power at what he often called its "capillaries." It does not have as much to do with Deleuze and Guattari's concept of micropolitics.

Deleuze and Guattari write, "the molecular, or microeconomics, micropolitics, is defined not by the smallness of its elements but by the nature of its 'mass' – the quantum flow as opposed to the molar segmented line."[8] It is not smallness but something else that defines the molecular and micropolitics. The quantum flow as opposed to the molar segmented line. What is a quantum flow? It is what we encountered in the discussion of science. A quantum flow is a virtual field that actualizes itself. It is a machinic process. Genetic information is a quantum flow. An egg is a quantum flow. Matter is a quantum flow, a fact we understand when we subject it to conditions that are far from equilibrium. In physics, quantum theory tries to understand matter as often being subject to chance and unpredictability. Einstein's quarrel with quantum theory concerns precisely this. "God does not play dice with the universe," he said. Oh, but God does, replied the quantum theorists, and Nietzsche and Deleuze with them. There is more to the universe than meets the eye, even the eye of the relativist.

Molar segmented lines: given identities with recognizable borders. Quantum flows: fluid identities that arise from a chaotic and often unpredictable folding, unfolding, and refolding of matter. Micropolitics is not an issue of the small; it is an issue of quantum flows. It is an issue of machines.

To think machinically is to recognize that the given identities of our political thought are more fluid and changeable than we have been led to believe. It is to seek not for the eternal nature of traditional political entities: the nation, the state, the people, the economy. It is instead

---

[8] Deleuze and Guattari, *A Thousand Plateaus*, p. 217.

to seek for what escapes them. This does not mean that one seeks for what lies outside of them; it means that one seeks for what escapes *from* them and *within* them. We no longer look for a transcendent or an outside. What escapes is of the same order as that which it escapes. There is only immanence. What Deleuze calls a *line of flight* is not a leap into another realm; it is a production within the realm of that from which it takes flight.

Political thought conceived in terms of the state or the economy is inadequate. It is inadequate because it is macropolitical thinking. But it is not macropolitical thinking because the state and the economy are large rather than small. They are large. But the inadequacy lies elsewhere. It is that thought oriented around them tends to be rigid. It lacks the suppleness that allows us to begin to recognize machinic processes. Deleuze and Guattari discuss the state and the economy. They discuss them at length. But only later, only after having established the primacy of the machinic, which is to say the micropolitical.

Are there no macropolitics? Are there no established identities that have bearing upon our political lives? There are: "everything is political, but every politics is simultaneously a *macropolitics* and a *micropolitics*."[9] We must be careful here, however. There are not two realms, the molar and the molecular, that intersect or collaborate to form a political creation. There are not even two separate levels. There is both a macropolitics and a micropolitics, but the micropolitics comes first. It is primary. Take, for example, the concept of social class:

social classes themselves imply "masses" that do not have the same kind of movement, distribution, or objectives and do not wage the same kind of struggle. Attempts to distinguish mass from class effectively tend toward this limit: the notion of mass is a molecular notion operating according to a type of segmentation irreducible to the molar segmentarity of class. Yet classes are indeed fashioned from masses; they crystallize them. And masses are constantly flowing or leaking from classes.[10]

Are there classes? Are there states? Are there sexes and modes of production and ethnic groups and national territories? Yes, there are. But we must think of these as relative stabilities, as products of machinic processes that at once construct them through the formation

9 Deleuze and Guattari, *A Thousand Plateaus*, p. 213.
10 Deleuze and Guattari, *A Thousand Plateaus*, p. 213.

of connections and overspill them from within. Macropolitics does exist, and we must study its processes if we are to understand the world in which we conduct our lives with others. But we must always keep in mind that while politics is simultaneously a macropolitics and a micropolitics, it is the micropolitics that is primary.

V

There are many political terms ahead of us: territorialization and deterritorialization, the state and capitalism, different kinds of lines (molar, molecular, lines of flight), subject groups and subjugated groups. Before turning to them, we should pause to take stock. The categories of the machine and of the macro- and micropolitical must find their place in the folds of Deleuze's thought.

The question we are asking is that of how one might live. It has been divided into two related questions: What might living consist in? How might we go about living?

To the first question, we have seen that living might be something that is not confined to organic matter. The world lives. Being lives. It lives not by organic processes but by unfolding its virtuality into actual forms, by realizing from within difference particular identities under particular conditions. Those identities do not cast themselves adrift from difference; they are suffused with difference. But identity is not *pure* difference; it is actualized difference.

Micropolitics is political thought that responds to difference. Traditional political thought has ossified. It can only reflect upon the identities it sees as eternal: the state, the nation, the economy, the military, and behind them all, the individual. But suppose these identities come later. Suppose they are not the primary items of politics. Suppose the world is indeed a world of difference. Then the individual, the state, the economy would be particular actualizations of a difference that need not be actualized in these particular ways, or that may be actualized in these ways but in many different ones as well.

Beneath this critique lies another one. It may be possible to conceive our political world in terms of these identities. Even though they are not primary, even though they are built upon a realm of supple differences, there may be nothing incoherent about using these identities to understand and modulate our relations with one another. Traditional liberal thought is not an impossible way of thinking about politics. It is not entirely wrongheaded or self-contradictory. Macropolitics captures, however inadequately, some aspects of our political experience. But if we substitute micropolitics for macropolitics, if we begin to think machinically, we begin to see more than macropolitics puts before our vision. Machines produce connections not only to the state and the economy. Machines produce all kinds of connections, connections that will only begin to be seen if we turn away from traditional political thought.

Consider the antiglobalization movement. If we look at it through the lens of traditional political theory, we may see something like this. Individuals have come together to resist certain effects of global capitalism on their lives and on the lives of others. Pollution, exploitation, destruction of natural resources, corruption of governments are all effects of global capitalism. By demonstrating, circulating petitions, raising awareness of the issue, the antiglobalization movement hopes to mitigate or perhaps end those effects, perhaps by ending capitalism as it has evolved over the past forty or fifty years.

This is not a mistaken view. There is something right in looking at the movement this way. There are, indeed, individuals coming together in the manner the description portrays. The problem is not that the account is false but that it is inadequate.

The first layer that this view fails to see is that people are connecting in ways that cut across traditional political categories. For example, organic farmers and antiglobalization activists are thinking about and practicing different ways of treating the earth and different approaches to eating. In this context, vegetarianism is a political activity. For another example, activist groups think about internal group dynamics. They ask how to relate to one another in ways that avoid domination or a repetition of traditional oppressions (of women, blacks, and so on). Rather than reproducing the traditional group structure of (usually white, male) leaders who create the agenda and followers who carry it out, they seek to allow for various or novel expressions, consensual decision making, and more active participation.

If we look at the antiglobalization movement strictly from the viewpoint of individuals forming organizations in order to intervene in standard political ways, we miss these other ways of connecting. Machinic thinking allows us to see them.

Deleuze uses a different example from recent traditional political thought. It is dated, but its very datedness is testimony to the agility he wants political thought to achieve.

imagine that between *the West and the East* a certain segmentarity is introduced, opposed in a binary machine, arranged in State apparatuses, overcoded by an abstract machine as a sketch of a World Order. It is then from *North to South* that the destabilization takes place.... A Corsican here, elsewhere a Palestinian, a plane hijacker, a tribal upsurge, a feminist movement, a Green ecologist, a Russian dissident – there will always be someone to rise up to the south.[11]

These different connections, which we might call "transversal" connections – since they cut across traditional political identities – are invisible to liberal political theory. Machinic thinking allows us to see them. Are these transversal connections political? They involve ways of living together; they involve power. Why would they not be political?

That is the first layer of politics traditional liberal thinking neglects. But there is another layer, or group of layers, to which machinic thinking will allow us access. For even at the first layer, we are dealing with individuals in relation to one another. And we need not approach, for example, the antiglobalization movement as a matter of individuals. We can look at it from other perspectives that will allow us to see different things.

Here is one of those other perspectives. The antiglobalization movement is a movement of the earth. It is a movement of some part of the earth seeking to renew itself in specific ways and to restore or protect other parts of the earth. The earth, we might say, consists in ecosystems. Those ecosystems may be in various kinds of balance; they may be *organic* in Claire Colebrook's sense of the term. But even when balanced, there are virtual imbalances inhabiting them. The antiglobalization movement is a particular type of imbalance cutting across ecosystems that attempts to protect or restore particular types of balance among them or within them. To anticipate some Deleuzian terms, the antiglobalization movement is a deterritorialization that will allow for a new type of reterritorialization.

What does looking at things this way allow us to see? Why should the earth be a political category? There are at least two insights we might

---

[11] Deleuze and Parnet, *Dialogues*, p. 131.

gain from giving an account that centers on the earth rather than upon individuals. First, it allows us to see that just as the environment is a political matter, politics as an environmental matter. Environmentalism is not simply a movement of individuals in relation to the earth. It is that, but it is not only that. Since individuals are themselves part of ecosystems, environmentalism is not only a movement *about* ecosystems but also a movement *within* them. Introducing the earth as a political category allows us to understand this.

Second, the shift from individuals to the earth loosens the grip traditional political categories have on our thought. Forcing ourselves to articulate the political by means of different categories reduces the sense of naturalness that attaches to those categories that have become ossified. It allows our thought an opportunity to gain or to regain suppleness. If we are to think politics by means of difference, we will need that suppleness.

This does not mean that we substitute the category of the earth for that of individuals in understanding the antiglobalization movement. It is not an either/or. As Deleuze often says in his later writings, it is and...and...and. We are not saying, "No, it's not about individuals, it's about the earth." We are saying, "Yes, it is about individuals, but no more about them than about the earth." The task is not one of replacing a single set of categories with another set. It is one of being able to create and move among various sets of categories, and even to cross between them. A political thought of difference recognizes that whatever categories we use, there is always more to say. We need to be prepared to switch perspectives in order to say more, in order to see more.

So far, we have been looking at the first reading of the question of how we might live: "What might living together consist of?" Deleuze and Guattari's machinic political approach allows us to open that question from different angles, to see different connections being made at different levels. Rather than taking it for granted that there are particular individuals with particular needs or lacks that the engagement in politics seeks to fill, political living might consist in the creation of connections among and within various actualized levels of difference: individuals, the earth, the South. Approaching the question this way opens up new paths for approaching the second question: "How might we go about living?"

In navigating this second question, we do not want to provide answers. We do not want to say, one should live in such and such a way. "There is no general prescription. We have done with all globalizing concepts."[12] It is not a question of how we *should* live; it is a question of how we *might* live. Seen from Deleuze and Guattari's viewpoint, the question might become something like this: "What connections might we form?" Or, "What actualizations can we experiment with?" If we ask the question this way, we need to bear in mind that the "we" of the questions is not a given we. It can be a group. It can be an individual. It can be an ecosystem or a pre-individual part or a cross-section within an environment or a geographical slice. What makes it a "we" is not the stability of an identity. It is the participation in the formation of connections.

Will this participation be a matter of living together? Will it involve power? Yes to both questions. Politics is an experiment in machinic connections; it is not a distribution of goods to those who lack them. To ask how we might go about living is not to repeat the dreary question of who needs what. It is instead to probe the realm of difference that we are in order to create new and (one hopes) better arrangements for living, in the broadest sense of the word *living*.

VI

There is another image Deleuze and Guattari use to characterize machinic thinking: rhizomatics. They contrast a rhizome with a tree. A tree has particular roots that embed themselves in the soil at a particular place and give rise to branches and then leaves in a particular way. It is a system of derivation: first the roots, then the trunk, then the leaves. The roots are embedded here and not elsewhere. The branches are bound to the trunk, the leaves to the branches.

Rhizomes do not work that way. Kudzu is a rhizome. It can shoot out roots from any point, leaves and stems from any point. It has no beginning: no roots. It has no middle: no trunk. And it has no end: no leaves. It is always in the middle, always in process. There is no particular shape it has to take and no particular territory to which it is

---

[12] Deleuze and Parnet, *Dialogues*, p. 144.

bound. It can connect from any part of itself to a tree, to the ground, to a fence, to other plants, to itself.

The tree is filiation, but the rhizome is alliance, uniquely alliance. The tree imposes the verb "to be," but the fabric of the rhizome is the conjunction, "and...and...and..." This conjunction carries enough force to shake and uproot the verb "to be." Where are you going? Where are you coming from? What are you heading for? These are totally useless questions.... *Between* things does not designate a localizable relation going from one thing to the other and back again, but a perpendicular direction, a transversal movement that sweeps one *and* the other way, a stream without beginning or end...[13]

Traditional political thought is arboreal: its thought is structured like a tree. First there is the individual, then the state, then the laws that answer back to the needs of the individual. Machinic thinking is rhizomatic. It allows for multiple connections from a variety of perspectives that are not rooted in a single concept or small group of concepts. Our political thought must be like kudzu. Only that way can it see beyond the single tree to which traditional liberal thought has tethered us. Only that way can living together be an exercise in creation rather than need reduction.

VII

Do Deleuze and Guattari, then, have nothing to say about the traditional political categories? Are there no individuals, no economic categories, no state in their politics? Can there be any intersection between the political thought they offer us and our other ways of conceiving politics, or do we have to start anew? Is politics, in their view, something other than what we have always been taught?

Deleuze and Guattari do talk of individuals, and of the state, and of capitalism. To understand this talk, however, requires a machinic orientation. Having developed this orientation, we are only now in a position to begin to think about more traditional political categories.

There are many ways to approach this thought. The one we will rely on here runs primarily through the last chapter of the *Dialogues*, which is co-authored by Deleuze and Claire Parnet and published in

[13] Deleuze and Guattari, *A Thousand Plateaus*, p. 25.

1977, between the publication of Deleuze and Guattari's two volumes of *Capitalism and Schizophrenia: Anti-Oedipus* and *A Thousand Plateaus*. The political thought developed in *Dialogues* is of a piece with that of the two major volumes, but its sustained discussion of politics is more accessible.

We are composed of lines. "Whether we are individuals or groups, we are made up of lines and these lines are very varied in nature. The first kind of line which forms us is segmentary – or rigid segmentarity... family-profession; job-holiday; family – and then school – and then the army – and then the factory – and then retirement."[14] Segmentary lines are themselves varied in nature. Certain kinds of lines are contemporaneous: family-profession. Other kinds are chronological: school-army-factory. The reason these lines are of a single type is that they are composed of categories we recognize, categories that might make up the elements of a traditional political theory. Segmentary lines are the lines with which traditional theory operates. As we saw before, Deleuze does not deny their existence. There are segmentary lines, and they are politically relevant. What Deleuze denies is their exclusive right to determine our political thought.

One might be uncomfortable with Deleuze's resort to segmentary lines. Given the discussion of language in Chapter 3, is it appropriate to see segmentary lines in operation anywhere? If linguistic categories are always overflowing themselves, then how can there be lines of rigid segmentarity? How can they be rigid? Don't they overflow themselves as well?

They do. Lines of rigid segmentarity are not rigid in the sense that nothing can get past them. We will see in a moment that these lines are composed of lines of flight whose nature is to overflow. What makes these lines rigid is not what they contain but what people *think* they contain. Lines of rigid segmentarity present themselves as rigid. They are infused with the dogmatic image of thought. "Relax, you're not at work now, you're on vacation," or, "Do you think you're still on vacation? Get focused; you're at work now."

It is not that these lines are not real. We *are* composed of lines of rigid segmentarity, just as there are cows and meadows in the world. But those lines, like cows and meadows, are more than they may seem.

[14] Deleuze and Parnet, *Dialogues*, p. 124.

The difficulty, for political thought and action, is to grasp that *more.* Otherwise, the fiction that there are only segmentary lines prevents us from seeing other ways of living. The idea that there are only segmentary lines becomes a politically self-fulfilling prophecy.

Deleuze calls lines of rigid segmentarity *molar.* These other lines he calls *molecular*:

we have lines of segmentarity which are much more supple, as it were molecular. . . . rather than molar lines with segments, they are molecular fluxes with thresholds or quanta. *A threshold is crossed, which does not necessarily coincide with a segment of more visible lines.* Many things happen on this second kind of line – becomings, micro-becomings, which don't even have the same rhythm as our "history."[15]

This sounds like the distinction between macropolitics and micropolitics that we have already seen. It is, but there is more. In moving from the molar to the molecular, we have passed from macropolitics to micropolitics. But there is still a third kind of line to be discussed that will also be a micropolitical one. Before turning to the third kind of line, we need to understand what a molecular line is.

We have already seen an example of it. The Palestinian, the Corsican, and the Green ecologist that rise up from the South are molecular figures. They cut across the divisions of the old political structure of East and West. They are representatives neither of Democracy and Capitalism nor the Triumph of Socialism. In some sense their politics is not foreign to us. After all, what Palestinians want involves things like autonomy and a separate state. However, their activity and their demands do not fit neatly into the geopolitical vision of East and West. Which is why, during the Cold War, they were often ignored or marginalized. (It is not a coincidence that Palestinians have often called themselves the Jews of the contemporary world. They have been the Other to those whose categories and concerns lie elsewhere.)

Molecular lines do not have the same rhythm as our "history." Our "history": the one we tell ourselves, the one we are taught to tell ourselves. Our "history" is the story of our names, our families, our jobs, our nation. Molecular lines have a different history, a history that runs

---

[15] Deleuze and Parnet, *Dialogues,* p. 124.

within and across the official one. "A profession is a rigid segment, but also what happens beneath it, the connections, the attractions and repulsions, which do not coincide with the segments, the forms of madness which are secret but which nevertheless relate to the public authorities."[16]

Earlier we saw that molecular lines, those drawn by the Palestinian or the Corsican, are still beholden to some traditional categories: the individual and the state. Beneath these lines, there is another set of lines: lines of flight. Lines of flight have two roles to play in Deleuze and Guattari's thought. They determine both molar lines and other types of molecular lines, and they offer other political adventures – and other political dangers.

"From the point of view of micropolitics, a society is defined by its lines of flight, which are molecular."[17] What is a line of flight, that molecular line that defines a society? It is the third kind of line, "which is even more strange: as if something carried us away, across our segments, but also across our thresholds, towards a destination which is unknown, not foreseeable, not pre-existent."[18]

We know what it sounds like, a line of flight. It sounds like an escape, a movement away from something. A convict on a prison break takes a line of flight. There is a prison; the convict flees it. That is a line of flight. Or so it seems.

This idea is not entirely wrong. There is something of the convict to a line of flight, and something of the prison to be escaped. But it misses the most important point. A society is defined by its lines of flight. Lines of flight do not escape from anything, or do not do only that. They are also constitutive. They define whole societies. How might they?

We are already prepared for this thought. Deleuze's ontology is an ontology of lines of flight. Lines of flight are the pure difference that lies beneath and within the constituted identities of segmentary lines and the partially constituted identities of molecular lines. They are not themselves constituted – or imprisoned – in specific identities. But they provide the material that will be actualized into those identities.

[16] Deleuze and Parnet, *Dialogues*, p. 125.
[17] Deleuze and Guattari, *A Thousand Plateaus*, p. 216.
[18] Deleuze and Parnet, *Dialogues*, p. 125.

Deleuze does not use the term *actualize* when he writes with Guattari. Instead he makes the distinction between *territorialization* and *deterritorialization*. A territorialized line is one that has a specific territory. It has been captured and imprisoned in a particular identity. There can be advantages to capture, to be sure. Capture is not all bad; it is a necessary moment of things. Territory needs to be marked out: statements need to be made, identities need to be constituted, people have to live somewhere. Or else there would be nothing but chaos, nothing but pure difference. Territorialization is not the enemy to be overcome. Or rather, it only becomes the enemy when we become blind to deterritorialization.

Deterritorialization is the chaos beneath and within the territories. It is the lines of flight without which there would be neither territory nor change in territory. Lines of flight are the immanent movement of deterritorialization that at once allows there to be a territory and destabilizes the territorial character of any territory.

A Marxist can be quickly recognized when he says that a society contradicts itself, is defined by its contradictions, and in particular by its class contradictions. We would rather say that, in a society, everything flees and that a society is defined by its lines of flight which affect masses of all kinds (here again, "mass" is a molecular notion). A society . . . is defined first by its points of deterritorialization, its fluxes of deterritorialization.[19]

We need to be clear here. The primacy of lines of flight is not chronological. It is not that there are first deterritorialized lines of flight and then later settled territories. There are always both: "the nomads do not precede the sedentaries; rather, nomadism is a movement, a becoming that affects sedentaries, just as sedentarization is a stoppage that settles the nomads."[20] The primacy of lines of flight is material. All material, whether territorial or deterritorialized, is constituted by lines of flight. Being is pure difference. There are always actualized identities, always territories. But those territories are rooted in deterritorialization, a deterritorialization that is not inert. It provides the resources for erasing and redrawing boundaries, for fleeing

[19] Deleuze and Parnet, *Dialogues*, p. 135.
[20] Deleuze and Guattari, *A Thousand Plateaus*, p. 430.

a particular territory for another one, and, under certain conditions, for imploding the territory itself.

It is the primacy of lines of flight that gives the machinic character to Deleuze's political thought. These lines are creative. They create territories and they create within territories. They are the element of segmentary lines and molecular lines. They are not organisms or mechanisms, but organisms and mechanisms contain them. And other organisms and mechanisms can be built from them. Seen from another perspective, they are the material of our living together, a material that forms and reforms itself in our living. It is a material that is at once the earth, the individual, the group, and the masses that flow within and across the earth, the individual, and the group. Together with molecular and segmentary lines, lines of flight are the stuff of our being and the proper focus of political thought. "In any case, the three lines are immanent, caught up in one another. We have as many tangled lines as a hand. We are complicated in a different way from a hand. What we call by different names – schizoanalysis, micro-politics, pragmatics, diagrammatism, rhizomatics, cartography – has no other object than the study of these lines, in groups or in individuals."[21]

It is in the thicket of these lines, in their entanglement, that we discover the state and capitalism.

VIII

We have seen the character of the state for traditional liberal thought. It is the referee between individuals, the mediator of their needs. It has a monopoly on the major power resources in a society, in order to prevent one set of interests from dominating another and oppressing it. But in the end that power must answer to the multiplicity of individual needs. The state is the arbiter of lack.

For Deleuze and Guattari, the state does not mediate, it creates resonances. "The State . . . is a phenomenon of *intraconsistency*. It makes points *resonate* together, points that are not necessarily already town-poles but very diverse points of order, geographic, ethnic, linguistic, moral, economic, technological particularities."[22] To create resonance

---

[21] Deleuze and Parnet, *Dialogues*, p. 125.
[22] Deleuze and Guattari, *A Thousand Plateaus*, p. 433.

is, first of all, to rely on something that precedes one. The state has no order of its own; it does not have its own reasons. The state is parasitic.

What is it parasitic on? Lines. It is parasitic on lines of flight, other types of molecular lines, and molar lines. But of the three, it is particularly from the molar lines that it draws its nourishment. Traditional thinking sees a state that answers – or at least ought to answer – to the needs of individuals. Deleuze and Guattari see a state that resonates molar lines. How does this happen?

Unlike molecular lines and especially lines of flight, molar lines have particular orders and identities. These orders and identities are not the same at all times and places. For one society, there may be an order that runs from son to warrior to farmer, while in another it may run from son to school child to graduate to professional. (And of course both those lines may exist in the same society.) But there is more. Not only are there orders and identities among the molar lines in a society, there are also what Deleuze and Guattari call *abstract machines.* They often credit Foucault with the analysis of abstract machines of power. Perhaps his most famous analysis of an abstract machine is that of discipline.

Discipline is not a creation of the state, although the state will have much to do with discipline. Discipline is a type of power that arises on the basis of diverse practices. It brings elements of each together to form a whole that in turn pervades nineteenth- and twentieth-century Western societies. This power is characterized by a minute observation of and intervention into the behavior of bodies, a distinction between the abnormal and the normal in regard to human desire and behavior, and a constant surveillance of individuals. For Foucault, the prison is the place where these characteristics first come together. They have migrated from the enclosure of the prison, however, infiltrating all corners of society. It is not that all power is reducible to disciplinary power; rather, it is that no part of society is immune to it. "Is this the new law of modern society?" Foucault asks of the idea of the normal that is at the heart of discipline. "Let us say rather that, since the eighteenth century, it has joined other powers – the Law, the Word and the Text – imposing new limitations on them."[23]

[23] Foucault, *Discipline and Punish*, p. 184.

We might think of discipline as an abstract machine. It does not exist as a concrete reality one could point to or isolate from the various forms it takes. Instead, it brings together diverse practices under a particular regime of power. One might say, with Deleuze and Guattari, that discipline, like other abstract machines, *overcodes* the molar lines of a society.

What is overcoding? It is the taking of diverse elements of power to pull them together into a particular arrangement that is then applied across large segments of society. Discipline arose through borrowing a variety of little power mechanisms. There were the precise time schedules of the monasteries, the practices of recording behavior and symptoms in hospitals, the enclosure of the emerging prison system, the experiments in military discipline in the Prussian army. These elements came together into a particular form of power that was then reapplied to hospitals, prisons, the military, and to schools and factories as well. In all these institutions there emerged a regimen of minute interventions into and recording of bodily movement in enclosed spaces on the basis of specific, detailed time schedules. Discipline overcoded these diverse practices.

The state enters at the point of overcoding. It reinforces overcoding and helps spread it to all corners of society. If an abstract machine is built from the resonance of a variety of molar lines, the state helps develop and maintain that abstract machine. "There are no sciences of the State but there are abstract machines which have relationships of interdependence with the State. That is why, on the line of rigid [that is, molar] segmentarity, one must distinguish the *devices of power* which code diverse segments, the *abstract machine* which overcodes them and regulates their relationships and the *apparatus of the State* which realizes this machine."[24] The state does not create the abstract machines; it realizes them. To create something, at least in this sense, is to bring it into being. By contrast, to realize something is to pull together into a whole what already exists in a more dispersed way.

[24] Deleuze and Parnet, *Dialogues*, p. 130. We have been talking here as though there were only one type of abstract machine, the type that overcodes molar lines. In *A Thousand Plateaus*, Deleuze and Guattari posit another type of abstract machine, "an abstract machine of mutation, which operates by decoding and deterritorialization." p. 223 This second type of abstract machine relies on lines of flight. The struggle between these two machines is that between overcoded molar identities and the lines of flight that both constitute and escape those identities.

Societies are complex entities, shot through with various intersecting molar lines, molecular lines, and lines of flight. How could an abstract machine take hold of various practices in society and maintain itself without some larger force that keeps it in place? The state is that larger force. "The State is not a point taking all the others upon itself, but a resonance chamber for them all."[25] In discipline, the state provides the resources to ensure that discipline can spread through and get a grip upon various social sectors. It provides the funding for large prisons, the organization for the military, the informational base for many hospitals, the structure of school systems. Without the state, it is hard to imagine how an abstract machine could take hold of the variety of practices it does. It is hard to imagine how something like an abstract machine could be installed in the midst of the complex relations of identity and difference that Deleuze and Guattari think are the material arrangements of any society. The state, although parasitic, is a necessary feature of a society that expects to maintain order through the imposition of uniformity across its surface.

We are far removed here from the liberal state that mediates the needs of individuals. The state, in Deleuze and Guattari's eyes, does not mediate. It does not use its monopoly on the means of force in order to prevent one set of individual interests from dominating another. Instead the state is by nature oppressive. It is a force for conformity. As traditional liberal theory recognizes, the state possesses enormous resources. But those resources are not in the service of mediation or liberation; they are in the service of a realization of the power of abstract machines and their oppression and conformity. The state realizes discipline. It creates the conditions under which abstract machines can reinforce the identity of molar lines and subject them to the same sorts of routines. The state is parasitic, powerful, and oppressive. And it has a strange relationship to capitalism.

IX

One might think that capitalism is another kind of abstract machine whose power is realized in the resonance chamber of the state. After

[25] Deleuze and Guattari, *A Thousand Plateaus*, p. 224.

all, does not capitalism bring together a variety of practices under the rubric of the market, which then overcodes those practices so that everything becomes a commodity? Is not the power of capital that of borrowing from a variety of economic practices and subjecting them to the conformity of the marketplace? And is not the role of the state to ensure capitalism's smooth operation, protecting its expansion and eliminating or marginalizing those that would stand in its way?

For many Marxists, this is the nature of capitalism and the role of the state. Capitalism is an abstract machine of exploitation. It steals from the workers the rightful fruits of their labor. The state serves this exploitation. It supports mechanisms whose ultimate goal is domination by a capitalist economic system. The overcoding realized by the state is in the service of the overcoding created by capitalism. The market prevails; it is supported by systems like those of discipline in order to maximize productivity and minimize resistance.

For Deleuze and Guattari, this story about capitalism and its relationship with the state lacks nuance. Like Marx himself, their relationship to capitalism is ambivalent. They credit capitalism for removing many past oppressions, for overthrowing mechanisms of conformity characteristic of our earlier history. On the other hand, capitalism creates its own damages. These damages must be understood and overthrown. Deleuze and Guattari are not simple Marxists; but they are hardly apologists for capitalism.

Think of the kinds of oppression capitalism has helped overcome. We are no longer bound to public authorities, our social surroundings, or even to our families in the way we once were. Kings do not rule us in the name of a higher power that presses us into submission. The church, the synagogue, the mosque are no longer the arbiters of our moral lives. We are no longer merely cogs in a larger social scheme that requires our unquestioning obedience. As Deleuze and Guattari put it, the old "codes" that have ruled us have been swept away by capitalism. They have been replaced instead by an "axiomatic."

The difference between an axiomatic and the codes it has replaced is described by Deleuze and Guattari this way:

the axiomatic deals directly with purely functional elements and relations whose nature is not specified, and which are immediately realized in highly varied domains simultaneously; codes, on the other hand, are relative to those

domains and express specific relations between qualified elements that cannot
be subsumed by a higher formal unity (overcoding) except by transcendence
and in an indirect fashion.[26]

Codes are concrete principles and rules that regulate specific people's
relationships with other specific people. An axiomatic is more abstract.
It regulates, but not through specific rules and not by means of specific
relationships.

Consider this historical change. At one time, peasants were tied to
the land and to the lord for whom they worked. They had a specific set
of obligations to that lord, obligations they had toward no other lord.
They could not pick up and move to the land of another lord, and
not simply because they could not afford to move or to buy land. The
idea of affording to move or buy land hardly existed in the world of
peasantry. One lived bound within a set of obligations to land and lord
that could be regulated or overcoded from a distance by the state, but
only by transcendence rather than immanence: only by imposition of
a force outside the specific relationship rather than part of it.

Contemporary laborers in a capitalist economy are in a very different situation. There is no bond of obligation to employer, no sanction
against moving. Laborers can move as they please as long as they can
afford it. They can buy land or equipment, invest capital, start up their
own businesses. There is no regulation of their relationships with specific others in a society.

This does not mean that they are free. Far from it. Even if we except
for the moment the overcoding realized by the state, capitalism has its
own ways of regulating behavior and interaction. The most prominent
among these ways has to do with the dominance of exchange value.
Marx's famous distinction between use value and exchange value is a
distinction between what an object can be used for and what it can
be exchanged for. In capitalism, it is exchange value rather than use
value that dominates. An object is worth what it can be exchanged for.
And these objects need not be material things: they can be ideas, or
labor, or self-respect.

Exchange value works as an axiomatic rather than as a code. It regulates not by setting rules between specific people or between people

[26] Deleuze and Guattari, *A Thousand Plateaus*, p. 454.

and things but by setting the manner in which all interactions can be governed. I can sell my labor to you; you can invest it in a product; you can sell that product to others; they can employ that product in their business to the extent that it allows them to create something that will afford them a favorable exchange with still others. In this chain, it is irrelevant who I am or who you are. I can be a laborer or a consultant or a doctor or lawyer. My position does not matter. The axiomatic is a functional regulator of relationships among diverse people and things. It can work across a variety of domains and does not respect (or restrict) people to specific offices or positions.

This is not, in Deleuze and Guattari's view, an entirely bad thing. Capitalism deterritorializes, clearing the ground for new ways of creating lives: "capitalism and its break are defined not solely by decoded flows, but by the generalized decoding of flows, the new massive deterritorialization, the conjunction of deterritorialized flows."[27] By deterritorializing previous territorialities, lines of flight are freed to travel to new territories, intersect with other lines of flight, engage in new experiments.

Unfortunately, that is not what happens in capitalism. Although possessed of a dynamic of deterritorialization, although decoding the flows with which it operates, capitalism has ways of ensuring that those decoded flows serve its own purposes. It has mechanisms of capture that stifle the flight of molecular lines.

One of these ways of stifling flight is the regime of discipline Foucault describes. Another, according to Deleuze and Guattari, is the Oedipus complex. Oedipus, like discipline, is an abstract machine that functions under capitalism to capture lines of flight and prevent them creating new ways of living. Deleuze and Guattari wrote *Anti-Oedipus* at the time of the ascendance of psychoanalysis in France. In their view, the idea of the family drama that Oedipus implies is a mechanism that focuses on desire. A desire is a line of flight. It is capable of creating new ways of living. But if its energy can be turned back upon itself – if it can be made to become entangled in itself – then its creativity will be inhibited. It will be put instead in the service of the dominant order, in this case the axiomatic of capitalism.

---

[27] Deleuze and Guattari, *Anti-Oedipus*, p. 224.

That is what Oedipus does. It turns desire centripetally back toward the family instead of allowing it to move centrifugally, experimenting with new connections.

Oedipus is the entangler of lines of flight. Rather than opening them to their own experiments, Oedipus says that your desires, your lines of flight, are really directed toward your own family. Whatever you think you desire, it is really your mother or your father you want. Lines of flight are captured, blocked from exploiting the deterritorialization that the emergence of capitalism affords. In that way, lines of flight can be placed in the service of capital rather than freed to pursue other directions. Familial molar lines replace older political codes as a means of capture for lines of flight. Capitalism retains its hegemony over the uncertain adventures that might follow the deterritorialization it has helped foster.

To many of us, the idea of Oedipus as a mechanism of capture may seem provincial or dated. The fortunes of psychoanalysis, never high in the United States or Britain, have fallen over the years. By the time Deleuze and Guattari publish the second volume of *Capitalism and Schizophrenia*, eight years after *Anti-Oedipus*, Oedipus is no longer a figure in their thought. Although the abstract machine of discipline continues to be recognized as a powerful mechanism binding lines of flight, Oedipus does not.[28] Now the capitalist axiomatic is directly exploitative. It does not require an intermediary.

The four principal flows that torment the representatives of the world economy, or the axiomatic, are the flow of matter-energy, the flow of population, the flow of flood, and the urban flow. The situation seems inextricable because the axiomatic never ceases to create all of these problems, while at the same time its axioms, even multiplied, deny it the means of resolving them (for example, the circulation and distribution that would make it possible to feed the world).[29]

---

[28] Near the end of his life, Deleuze begins to question whether discipline is still effective as an abstract machine. He suggests that we have moved from a society of discipline to a society of control, characterized not by the confinement and regulation of bodies but by "ultrarapid forms of apparently free-floating control that are taking over from the old disciplines at work within the time scales of closed systems." "Postscript on Societies of Control," p. 178.

[29] Deleuze and Guattari, *A Thousand Plateaus*, p. 468.

There is no Oedipus here. The capitalist axiomatic creates its own difficulties, engages in its own oppression. By submitting all flows to the regime of exchange value, capitalism reterritorializes the lines of flight it has freed from previous codes. It binds them to an axiomatic that keeps them within the orbit of capitalism without requiring an outside force to intervene. In this situation, Oedipus is no longer required.

Does the state have a role to play here? It does, although its role is more limited than it was in earlier regimes. "What characterizes our situation is both beyond and on this side of the State."[30] Even without Oedipus, though, there are other abstract machines at work (for example, discipline) that require the resonance of the state in order to be maintained. Moreover, to think of a society as reducible to its economic arrangements is to deny the complexity of its composition. Not all molar lines are in service of the economy. And molar lines are themselves composed of lines of flight that are more than the molar lines they constitute.

Perhaps we are living in a world where states hold less sway over the societies they are said to govern. Perhaps the development of capitalism does not require the support of the state to the degree it did in the nineteenth century and in most of the twentieth century. This does not mean that states will wither away. There will always be lines of flight, pressing against the territorializations of the moment. There will always be abstract machines seeking to capture, entangle, or constrict those lines of flight. And there will always be a need to realize and maintain those abstract machines by making their elements resonate across social arrangements. Whether in the service of capitalism or not, states are not poised at the edge of disappearance.

The story many Marxists tell about the relation of capitalism to the state, the story we cited a few pages ago, is not entirely wrong. The state does overcode society in the service of capitalism. But the story is not entirely right, either. An account that focuses solely on the state's service to a purely exploitative capitalism misses the complexity of both state and capitalism. The state is not only in the service of capitalism; its overcoding touches on aspects of our lives that are not reducible to economics. And capitalism is not purely exploitative. The

[30] Deleuze and Parnet, *Dialogues*, p. 146.

axiomatic that binds us to the market also frees us from the oppression of traditional social codes. The question facing us now, the political question, is how to mobilize the deterritorialization that capitalism unleashes in the service of new ways of living together.

X

How might we conceive resistance to the capitalism's axiomatic and the state's resonance of overcoding? How might we begin to think about mobilizing lines of flight in order to create alternative social arrangements? At the end of Chapter 3, we saw that to think differently is not a solitary activity. It is difficult, if not impossible, to do on one's own. And to live differently on one's own is more difficult still. Deleuze has offered us an ontology that responds to difference. Deleuze and Guattari have carried that ontology into the realm of politics. How might we use this ontology and this politics in the project of living together? How might we release our lines of flight, recover the machines coiled within the organisms and mechanisms?

In *Anti-Oedipus*, Deleuze and Guattari distinguish between *subject groups* and *subjected groups*. Each involves an investment of desire. But both involve very different investments.

Every investment is collective, every fantasy is a group fantasy and in this sense a position of reality. But the two kinds of investment are radically different, according as the one bears upon the molar structures that subordinate the molecules, and the other on the contrary bears upon the molecular multiplicities that subordinate the structured crowd phenomena. One is a *subjected group* investment . . . which socially and psychically represses the desire of persons; the other, a *subject-group* investment in the transverse multiplicities that convey desire as a molecular phenomenon . . . [31]

Subjected groups and subject groups. Subjected groups think and act in terms of molar lines, machines and organisms. Their world consists solely of actualities, never of virtualities that might be actualized. It is not difficult to find subjected groups engaged in politics. Turn on the television. The talking heads will offer subjected group talk to anyone willing to listen. There is always an *us* and a *them*. The distinction is

---

[31] Deleuze and Guattari, *Anti-Oedipus*, p. 280.

clearly drawn. There are things *we* can do to *them*, or at least ways *we* can help *ourselves*, but *we* must be realistic. We can debate the options, but when one of them is chosen, we must fall in behind it. Everyone has a role to play. Mothers should be mothers; workers should contribute in the way of their work; children should listen to their parents.

This is the thought of subjected groups: clear distinctions among molar lines with already understood goals. It is pure Nietzschean reactivity. But recall what Deleuze said about philosophy. "It is a question of someone – if only one – with the necessary modesty not managing to know what everybody knows." That is where subject groups begin. With subject groups, it is not only one. Every investment, Deleuze and Guattari tell us, is collective. We are never alone, not in our molar lines and not in our molecular lines. It *is* a question of some among *us* not managing to know what the rest of us know. Subject groups are ignorant. Like Socrates, their wisdom lies in knowing that they do not know. And most important, they do not yet know what their collective bodies are capable of.

To be ignorant is not to be stagnant. It is not to be paralyzed. To be ignorant in this way is instead to be seeking new possibilities, new formations. It is to be creating new connections. It is to move among the as yet undecided and the undecidable in order to see what might be created. "Every struggle is a function of all these undecidable propositions and constructs *revolutionary connections* in opposition to the *conjugations of the axiomatic*."[32] Machines connect; they do not conjugate within an axiomatic, but create new connections with other machines. They actualize new moments of the virtual. Fail to know what everyone else knows and you have a chance to create something interesting. Never alone, always in a group. Groups do not have to be stifling. They do not have to be subjected groups. Find others who are willing to touch the virtual and you have a subject group.

Deleuze often talks of nomads and minorities. He contrasts nomads with sedentaries. We have seen that there are always both nomads and sedentaries. Deleuze throws in his lot with the nomads, with those whose restlessness sends them on strange adventures, even when those adventures happen in a single place, as they do for writers and philosophers. Nomads do not know. They seek. They seek not to find

[32] Deleuze and Guattari, *A Thousand Plateaus*, p. 473.

something, because there is not a something to be found. There is no transcendence to comfort them. They seek not to discover but to connect. Which is to say they seek to create. They palpate the virtual in their work in order to discover what may be connected to it. They embrace the eternal return, because it will always offer them something they do not know. They are not afraid to throw the dice, and are not fearful of the dice that fall back.

Minorities are nomadic adventures. To become minor is to seek to connect with neglected movements in the social body. These connections can be political in the traditional sense, but they do not need to be. They can be artistic, culinary, vocational, linguistic, scientific, parental, or literary. Deleuze and Guattari's book on Kafka is a book about a writer seeking to become minor, in part through the use of a particular variant of German. "Prague German is a deterritorizalized language, appropriate for strange and minor uses. (This can be compared in another context to what blacks in America today are able to do with the English language.)"[33]

To become minor is not to embrace a particular identity, and it has nothing to do with how many are in the group compared with the number in the majority. Becoming-woman is a becoming minor, even if there are more women than men. To become minor is to jostle the reins of the majority identity in order to investigate new possibilities, new ways of becoming that are no longer bound to the dominant molar lines and their abstract machines. It is to investigate the virtual whose vision is often obscured by the molar lines of the majority. It is to break with identity, which is always the identity of the majority, in favor of difference as yet unactualized. As Deleuze and Guattari say of Kafka, "A minor literature doesn't come from a minor language; it is rather that which a minority constructs within a major language."[34]

Ebonics is not a different language. It is English, twisted into unrecognizable forms in order to express different experiences. It is not another language but an experiment in language, one that breaks from the major language of English in order to say new things or create new rhythms or utter new sounds. Once Ebonics develops its own

---

[33] Deleuze and Guattari, *Kafka: Toward a Minor Literature*, p. 17.
[34] Deleuze and Guattari, *Kafka*, p. 16.

codes and rules, it becomes a major language, even if only African-Americans speak it. As John Rajchman says,

Minor languages like Black English pose this problem – one must devise ways of being at home not in a territory but in this Earth, which, far from rooting them in a place, an identity, a memory, releases them from such borders and becomes light or deterritorialized, like a tent put down by nomads.... The problem is no longer that of "the people," but of "a people," an indefinite people, as yet "without qualities," still to be invented...[35]

Nomadism and minorities are not the activities solely of particular individuals banding together. They may be that, but they do not have to be. Nomadism and becoming-minor can happen across groups or even at a pre-individual level. The behavior of particular chemicals at far from equilibrium conditions is a becoming-minor, an actualization of a neglected aspect of the virtual field. The emergence of the antiglobalization movement is a becoming-minor of many different groups with a variety of particular goals and purposes; their convergence on issues of exploitation, eating, and group decision making are a becoming-minor of traditional political processes (and, like all becomings-minor, in perpetual danger of evolving into a new code proclaiming How Things Should Be).

None of the terms Deleuze and Guattari introduce – subject groups, nomads, minorities – offers a specific political agenda. "There is no general prescription. We are done with all globalizing concepts." If you ask them, "What should we do now?" they will not offer you an answer. Or, if they offer one, it will look like this:

This is how it should be done: Lodge yourself on a stratum, experiment with the opportunities it offers, find an advantageous place on it, find potential movements of deterritorialization, possible lines of flight, experience them, produce flow conjunctions here and there, try out continuums of intensities segment by segment, have a small plot of new land at all times.... Connect, conjugate, continue: a whole "diagram," as opposed to still signifying and subjective programs.[36]

Is that an answer to the question of what should be done or merely a call to arms? It is both. What Deleuze and Guattari point to here

---

[35] Rajchman, *The Deleuze Connections*, pp. 95–6.
[36] Deleuze and Guattari, *A Thousand Plateaus*, p. 161.

are not political programs but ways of conceiving and acting upon our experience. We understand these terms: deterritorialization, lines of flight, continuums of intensities. What we need to do now is think and act by means of them. This does not require an avant-garde to tell us where our interests lie. It rejects the crutch of an avant-garde. It places responsibility in our hands, as long as we understand the word *our* to refer not to individuals nor to pre-individual objects nor to groups nor to states nor to organizations nor to transversal alignments but to all of these, each at its proper level and in its proper context.

And, a final point, and perhaps the most important one, politics is an experiment, not a deduction. If we had not known this before, the history of the twentieth century should have taught it to us. There are no formulas, no rules, no programs that can be imposed from above. To think otherwise is to invite abuse and slaughter in the name of ideals that often prove to be at once noble and empty, or base and empty, but in any case empty. Deleuze and Guattari teach us much of what is wrong with our political world. They offer us ways to conceive ourselves and our being together that allow us to begin to experiment with alternatives. *But there is no general prescription.* There are only analyses and experiments in a world that offers us no guarantees, because it is always other and more than we can imagine. We roll the dice; we do not know for sure what will fall back. "Everything is played in uncertain games.... The question of the future of the revolution is a bad question because, in so far as it is asked, there are so many people who do not *become* revolutionaries, and this is exactly why it is done, to impede the question of the revolutionary-becoming of people, at every level, in every place."[37]

Everything is played in uncertain games. Each line has its own dangers. The dangers of molar lines are obvious. They have been detailed by Deleuze, Guattari, and Foucault. But molecular lines have their dangers as well. "It is not sufficient to attain or trace out a molecular line ... it is the supple lines themselves which produce or encounter their own dangers, a threshold crossed too quickly, an intensity become dangerous because it could not be tolerated ... a supple line rushes into a black hole from which it will not be able to extricate

[37] Deleuze and Parnet, *Dialogues*, p. 147.

itself."[38] Molecular lines can paint themselves into a corner. Perhaps that is what the proponents of identity politics in the United States did in the 1980s. In seeking to articulate particular political identities (gayness, blackness) from which to address their oppressions, they wound up isolating groups from one another, ghettoizing progressive politics rather than mobilizing it.

The dangers associated with lines of flight are "perhaps the worst of all. It is not just that lines of flight, the most steeply sloping, risk being barred, segmentarized, drawn into black holes. They have yet another special risk: that of turning into lines of abolition, of destruction, of others and of oneself."[39] Deleuze cites examples of this danger in literature: F. Scott Fitzgerald and Virginia Woolf among them. Follow a line of flight and you do not know where it leads. It could lead anywhere or nowhere at all. It could lead to its own obliteration.

Our task in politics is not to follow the program. It is not to draft the revolution or to proclaim that it has already happened. It is neither to appease the individual nor to create the classless society. And it does not lie in the slogan "To the molecular, to the lines of flight." Our task is to ask and answer afresh, always once more because it is never concluded, the question of how one might live. It is a question we ask and answer not solely with our words or our thoughts but with our individual and collective lives, in an experimentation that is neither guaranteed nor doomed but always in the process of becoming.

---

[38] Deleuze and Parnet, *Dialogues*, p. 138.
[39] Deleuze and Parnet, *Dialogues*, p. 140.

5

Lives

I

John Coltrane was a jazz saxophonist. He was born in North Carolina
in 1926 and died in New York in 1967. In between, he produced
some of the most influential music in the history of jazz. Alongside
Louis Armstrong, Duke Ellington, Charlie Parker, Miles Davis, and
Thelonious Monk, Coltrane stands as a peer. There is no jazz saxophonist playing today that does not stand in his shadow. The question
for many young saxophonists is whether he left any light for them.

Coltrane did not have the struggle of many jazz musicians to be
recognized. Although he put in his time in bars and juke joints, at a
fairly young age he was able to play with many of the top jazz bands
of the time, including those of Miles Davis and Thelonious Monk. It
was during the collaborations with Miles and Monk that he began to
develop his own sound.

In some of his live music recorded in the late 1950s, one can hear
its beginnings. Coltrane's solos became longer, more searching. It was
as though he were experimenting with different ways of approaching a song, now this way and now that, often during the same solo.
Miles Davis once said that when he asked Coltrane about the length
of his solos, Coltrane said that he didn't know how to stop playing.
(Davis's reply was, reportedly, "Take the horn out of your mouth.") The
solos also became more intense, with more notes covered and faster
runs. To listen to Davis and Coltrane play together was to hear a study

in contrasts: Davis's spare playing sought the single right note for a particular musical space, while Coltrane filled the air with what came to be called his "sheets of sound."

In 1960 Coltrane formed his own group. At first the group played within the recognized context of the jazz of the time, hard bop. But during the early 1960s, other influences began to find their way into the music. Coltrane described having a "spiritual awakening" in 1957, and his music of the early 1960s showed traces of a more spiritual nature. While incorporating sources as diverse as slave spirituals and Indian classical music, Coltrane moved away from hard bop jazz into something still more searching and restless. His solos became longer still and, for many of his listeners, mesmerizing. He often substituted for the tenor saxophone the higher pitched soprano, an instrument played by Sidney Bechet in the 1920s and 1930s, but rarely used since. Videotapes of concerts in the 1960s show Coltrane tethered to his horn, eyes tightly shut, playing wave after wave of notes while his band pushed the music from behind. It was as though he became a dervish, lost to the sound, immersed in, rather than creating, it.

It was not exactly like that, however. Even when he was most involved in the music, he was still seeking to push it further, to discover what it could do. His drummer, Elvin Jones, recalled an occasion on which Coltrane put down his saxophone and started beating his chest in front of the microphone, trying to create sounds that lay outside the range of his horn.

By the mid-1960s Coltrane was experimenting in the "free jazz" of the time, playing atonal music that even many of his devoted listeners found difficult to follow. He brought in new musicians, people playing on the margins of jazz, in order to experiment with those margins himself. One of his late albums, "Ascension," remains among the most challenging of jazz compositions. Its sound is cacophonous, dispersed, intense without respite. In keeping with the album's title, it is as though Coltrane were seeking to force a spiritual ascension through the sheer force of the instruments, as though another effort, just one more, might land them all in another realm.

Near the end of his life, those around Coltrane described his frequent bouts of exhaustion. He would take breaks from playing, but each one was followed by a more intense musical quest. He died at the age of forty-one of a liver ailment that was probably exacerbated by the intensity of his involvement in the music.

How might we understand Coltrane's musical itinerary?

Here is one way. Coltrane was seeking something transcendent, using the music to attain a spiritual state that was beyond the music, raising his listeners along with him to that state. The advantage of this way of understanding it is that it seems to conform to some of Coltrane's own, religiously tinged, descriptions of what he was seeking to accomplish. The disadvantage of this way of understanding it is that it neglects the *music*. The music, on this description, is a means to an end. The fact that it was music and not painting or writing is irrelevant.

Coltrane was once asked what he would do if he could no longer play music. He replied that music was all he knew how to do.

There is another, better way to describe what Coltrane was doing. It starts with the music. Music is a virtual field of differences that can be actualized in many different ways. It is a rich virtual field, one that, if its history is any indication, is inexhaustible. Unfortunately, most musicians do not touch the virtual. They do not even seek to. The recording industry is not an investigator of music's virtuality; it is a purveyor of its most common and banal identities. And most musicians, seeking to sell albums, are content to confine their musical journeys to the boundaries of current public taste. Even what count as transgressions in contemporary music – provocative lyrics or stage props or clothing – are little more than titillations rather than musical developments.

Coltrane refused the confines of any particular musical context. This was not because he was rebelling against them. Some people describe the intensity of his music as angry, but most who listen to him think of it as ecstatic. The one overtly political piece that he did compose, "Alabama," created in the wake of the bombing of a Birmingham church in which four children were killed, is a dirge rather than a protest. Coltrane was not reactive, in the Nietzschean sense. He did not resent the music industry (which was more supportive of alternative music then); nor did he seem to feel burdened by the dominant structures of the music of his day.

Rather then rebel, Coltrane created. And his particular form of creation was to see what *more* there could be in the music he played.

He did not so much compose or arrange or express; he searched. He threw the dice. His playing was an active force, going to the limit of what it could do. He investigated to see what else the music might contain that it had not shown before. He played not to display the actual but to touch the virtual. And since he was a jazz musician, his form of touching the virtual was largely improvisational. Unlike Schoenberg, for instance, who created the twelve-tone scale, Coltrane's investigation into the virtual of music happened while he played rather than while he composed.

Looked at as an investigation of the virtual rather than as a step into transcendence, Coltrane's itinerary makes more sense. It puts the music in the center of the account, rather than seeing it as a means. But we need to say more. As yet, the figure of John Coltrane is too distinct from the music. We need to recognize that Coltrane was as much a vehicle for the music as he was its master. This is why his relation to the music was one of searching rather than expression. The music played itself through him as much as he played it. At the moment of improvisation, there is in fact only a single entity: Coltrane-music. As Deleuze puts the more general point, "The life of the individual gives way to an impersonal and yet singular life that releases a pure event freed from the accidents of internal and external life, from the subjectivity and objectivity of what happens: a 'Homo tantum' with whom everyone empathizes and who attains a sort of beatitude."[1]

In improvisational jazz, we can see this clearly. Coltrane practiced up to eight hours a day. He sought out different forms of music, different types of musical scales, different musicians to talk to. The end of this practice and this seeking was not to master the music but to be able, at the moment of playing, to allow the virtual of music to actualize itself through his saxophone. It was in the music, not beyond it, that the beatitude lay.

II

On the afternoon of December 8, 1987, an Israeli truck hit a car carrying Palestinian laborers, killing four of them. This was not the

---

[1] Deleuze, "Immanence: A Life," p. 28.

first time Palestinian workers had been killed by Israelis. To the contrary, that Israelis were killing Palestinians was not surprising to anybody. Whether this particular killing was intentional or not was never discovered. Given what happened afterwards, it did not much matter.

Demonstrations began almost immediately after the killing, starting in the populous Gaza refugee camp of Jebalya, and spread throughout the occupied territories. Young Palestinian males, armed with no more than rocks, confronted Israeli tanks, machine guns, and tear gas. At first, it looked like the kind of outburst that is common among oppressed populations: an explosion of rage, soon followed by the return of quiescent despair.

This time, however, the quiescence did not return. Demonstrations continued; they gained in intensity. An underground leadership emerged, the United National Leadership, issuing leaflets calling for demonstrations and strikes at particular times and places. The more the Israelis tried to put down the resistance, the more persistent it became. Soon the movement earned a name: *intifada*, an Arabic term that means rising up or casting off.

As media coverage around the world continued to show images of a technologically advanced army pitted against stone-throwing youths in their own streets and villages, Israel became desperate to end the intifada. Defense Minister Yitzhak Rabin announced a policy of "force, might, and beatings." The application of that policy was shown on television, which increased both Palestinian resistance and world outrage at Israel's behavior. Less publicly, Israel tried to divide the Palestinian community. In a move it was later to regret, Israeli officials encouraged the rise of the Islamic group Hamas as a counterweight to the PLO, who it thought was behind the uprising. Although Hamas created some division within the movement, for instance calling for strikes on different days from the United National Leadership, there was no diminishing of the intifada's energy.

As it unfolded, the intifada took on different aspects. It was not solely a matter of confronting the military aspect of occupation, but of developing self-reliance, national pride, and a sense of the future. Day care centers sprang up that taught Palestinians their history and cultural legacy, something that had been neglected in the Israeli-supervised schools. National symbols, such as the banned Palestinian flag, were displayed on telephone lines and spray-painted on building walls. Women's agricultural collectives were formed, planting and harvesting crops. Small backyard gardens sprang up, providing food that was passed from house to house during the weeklong curfews imposed by Israel. Professors held classes in secret in their homes after the Israeli army closed Palestinian universities.

Perhaps no one was more surprised by the intifada – its range, its intensity, its longevity – than the Palestinians themselves. In the United States, Palestinians are seen as an unruly people drawn toward terrorism. This image does not match the history of the Palestinian people. On the contrary. Palestinians are often embarrassed by their own lack of political will. In 1948, when nearly three-quarters of a million of them were driven off their land by Israeli forces, they went quietly, with little resistance except for a few irregular armed groups. From 1948 until 1967 they were ruled by Jordan in the West Bank and Egypt in the Gaza Strip. Aside from the formation of the PLO in 1964 there was little political initiative directed toward achieving a Palestinian state. During the first twenty years of the Israeli occupation of the West Bank and the Gaza Strip, from 1967 until 1987, Palestinian resistance was sporadic. There were long periods of calm punctuated by demonstrations or a hijacking or a terrorist attack. There was no broadbased popular movement.

It was not that there were no complaints. Palestinians in the refugee camps longed for a return to the land Israel had dispossessed them of in 1948. And Palestinians whose home was in the West Bank complained as their lands were confiscated for Israeli settlements and their livelihoods transformed into day labor for Israel. There were arbitrary arrests, house demolitions, daily humiliations, deportation, collective punishment, and Israeli terrorism against anyone who tried to resist the occupation. And there was occasional resistance. But until 1987, the idea of a mass popular resistance movement seemed foreign to the family- and agriculturally based Palestinian culture.

The intifada was not an entirely spontaneous affair. It did not arise, fully formed and articulated, from nowhere. There were structures already in place to take advantage of the killings of the Palestinian workers. For several years before the intifada, local organizers had been working in towns and villages to pull together a variety of underground organizations: resistance groups, self-help groups, medical groups, cultural education groups. But even those involved in the development of these groups were surprised by the speed with which events unfolded after December 8. The energy and will, the spontaneous coordination and resistance had little analogy in Palestinian history.

So what happened? We cannot say that the killings on December 8 were unusual, or especially egregious. They were not. There was nothing that happened on that day to distinguish it from many others. It would be more accurate to say that the killings precipitated a movement that was ready to happen, that this particular incident was a spark that touched the dry wood of Palestinian anger. But we must be careful here. It had been despair as much as anger that had been the most common Palestinian response to Israeli occupation. Why did things change so quickly?

We should recall two aspects of Prigogine's study of chemical reactions in conditions that are far from equilibrium. First, chemicals can display behavior for which there seems to be no causal explanation, for example the chemical clock. Second, small changes in the environment can have a decisive impact on the nature of a chemical change. Recall as well the lesson both Deleuze and Prigogine draw from this study: we should think of the chemical field not as one of identities in causal interaction but of differences that can be actualized in a variety of ways.

It would not be wrong to say of the Palestinians that they were capable of the intifada under the right conditions. But it would be misleading to say that the intifada was waiting to happen, and that December 8 just allowed it to emerge. To put things that way assumes that every Palestinian – or at least a good many of them – were waiting, consciously or unconsciously, for a moment to express their resistance. It assumes that resistance lay wholly formed in each Palestinian breast, anticipating its appointed hour. It was not like that. If it were, there would have been no surprise among the Palestinian organizers at the intifada's depth and intensity. The anger, the resentment, the sense of injustice and desire to resist: these were all more free-floating. They had not coalesced, at least in the minds of most Palestinians, into a particular determination. It was the unfolding events of December 1987 and January 1988 that arranged them in a particular way, that made them what they were to become.

The philosopher Ludwig Wittgenstein once said that it is in speaking that we discover what it is that we want to say.[2] In the intifada, it was in action that the Palestinians discovered their ability to resist. What we later call resistance is not a particular identity lying nascent in previous conditions, but an aspect of the virtual that assumes a particular identity when it is actualized. It is correct to say of the Palestinians before December 8 that they were ripe for resistance; it is incorrect to say that the resistance was already there, waiting to be expressed. The former is a matter of difference, the latter an example of the dogmatic image of thought.

John Rajchman writes, "To say we each have 'a life' and to say that we each have *an* unconscious thus amounts to the same thing. It means that there is always something outside our 'identifications' as subject or persons, which we play out through complexifying encounters . . . "[3] The first Palestinian intifada had a life. It had an unconscious that was played out through the complexifying encounters that emerged during the weeks after December 8, 1987. The Palestinians did not think of themselves as a resistant people before then. (Largely they thought of themselves as an *enduring* people.) They were right. Before December 1987, Palestinians, *as a people*, were not resistant. Resistance was not there, waiting to be unleashed. Something was there, or, better, somethings were there. There were various elements – despair, pride, anger – that were not but could become resistance, depending on the unfolding of events.

Even to describe it that way, as though there were particular elements that needed only to be mobilized in order to become resistance, is misleading. Before I begin to speak, I do not know exactly what I want to say. There are no shards of thought, lying scattered in my consciousness, that need only to be pieced together by the adhesive of my words. Before the formation of a chemical clock, there are no potentialities for chemical concentration that lie in wait for an energy source to release them. Before Coltrane begins to play a solo, there

---

[2] " 'I was going to say. . . .' – You remember various details. But not even all of them together shew your intention. It is as if a snapshot of a scene had been taken, but only a few scattered details of it were to be seen . . . And now it is as if we knew quite certainly what the whole picture represented. As if I could read the darkness." Wittgenstein, *Philosophical Investigations*, p. 163.

[3] Rajchman, *The Deleuze Connections*, p. 89.

are no notes, neither in his mind nor in his horn. There is a virtual that he can draw upon in order to create notes, notes that follow one another in a coherent pattern that itself did not exist before he started to play.

To describe the emergence of the intifada as a mobilization of particular elements assumes that each of those elements has a particular identity, and that they only need to be arranged in the proper order for the intifada to happen. But elements change. What was anger becomes determination; what was despair becomes hope. There is always more going on than meets the eye. Everything is always more than its identity. *There is always something outside our identification as subjects and persons.* It was the unfolding relationships among elements that were more than merely elements that made the first intifada what it was. It was the actualization of the virtual, the unfolding of difference, that created the popular resistance that lasted until 1993.

There is another lesson here too, sadder in this case. Actualization does not guarantee the persistence of an identity. The eternal return is the return of difference, not identity. The second Palestinian intifada, the Al-Aksa intifada that started in September 2000,[4] has not been like the first. It has not been a movement of popular resistance but one engaged in by military elites with more passive popular support. The second intifada, although larger in scale than pre-1987 opposition, remains mostly an opposition of the resistance groups rather than of the Palestinian population itself. There are, perhaps, many reasons for this: exhaustion from the first intifada, continuing and further dispossession by Israel, corruption in Yassir Arafat's political regime, and the existence of military weaponry in the occupied territories that divides the population into those who have weapons and those who do not. In any case, the lesson for us is that the virtual remains coiled within the actual. Difference returns, identity is fragile. No particular arrangement, no particular state of folding and unfolding, good or bad, is ever secure. The truth will out, some have said. But nothing will necessarily out: not truth, not evil, not justice. There are no guarantees, except that there is more to come.

---

[4] The name "Al-Aksa intifada" derives from its precipitating event, the deliberately provocative visit of Ariel Sharon to the Temple Mount/Haram El-Sharif, where the Al-Aksa mosque is located.

III

In the 1950s and 1960s, American cities were subject to the clarion call of urban renewal. Urban renewal would deal with the decay of the cities, their dissolution and their blight. Faced with increasing poverty, crime, and congestion, urban renewal would counter the chaotic nature of the urban environment with planning and organization. There would be new roads and highways to accommodate traffic into and out of urban centers. There would be new high-rise housing for the poor that removed them from the dangers of street-level living. There would be distinct areas for shopping, for living, for entertainment, for work. Each area would have its own facilities and resources: a habitat for each aspect of urban life. Urban chaos would give way to an orderly city life.

It was all a spectacular failure.

Funds for roads and highways supplanted mass transit and increased automotive congestion in city centers. Low-income high-rise buildings further marginalized impoverished citizens and divided African-American and white populations, concentrating the ghetto rather than eliminating it. The separation of areas of life raised crime rates rather than lowering them, diminished urban life, and isolated city residents from one another. A city, it turns out, is not to be modeled on a suburb.

Jane Jacobs had already taught us this in 1961 with her book *The Death and Life of Great American Cities*. City planners want things arranged in neat patterns. Shops go over here, residences over there, and highways go through everything to add accessibility. But cities are not like that. Cities are messy affairs. They work not by an orderly segregation but by a more spontaneous integration of disparate factors. It is not that there is no order in cities. But urban order emerges from diversity, rather than the other way around.

This order is all composed of movement and change, and although it is life, not art, we may liken it to the dance – not to a simple-minded precision dance with everyone kicking up at the same time ... but to an intricate ballet in which the individual dancers reinforce each other and compose an orderly whole. The ballet of a good city sidewalk never repeats itself from place to place, and in any one place is always replete with new improvisations.[5]

---

[5] Jacobs, *The Death and Life of Great American Cities*, p. 50.

Here is what happens if you plan a city according to the doctrine of urban renewal. The residential areas do not have anyone walking around in them either during the day or the evening, because there is nowhere to go. People emerge from their homes in the morning to go to work and return to them in the late afternoon. If they leave their houses again, it is by car to go to another part of town. The business areas become deserted after dark, since there is no reason for anyone to be there except to work or shop. Relying on highways instead of mass transit further isolates people. People travel in their vehicular bubbles from home to work to entertainment and back to home. This is a recipe for desolate streets, high crime rates, and, consequently, flight from cities to suburbs.

It is worse in the high-rise ghetto. Concentrating impoverished populations in high-rises surrounded by access roads only serves to increase their isolation from the rest of the city. It reinforces people's staying in their apartments. And by keeping people away from one another, by diminishing community life, it invites crime.

The core of a city lies not in the number of people who live there but in the quality of its street life. This is the lesson of Jane Jacobs' urbanism. Consider, she asks us, a neighborhood that has residential, business, and entertainment elements woven together. There are people on the street at all hours. In the morning, people shop and go to work. In the afternoon, they stroll, eat lunch, and shop. In the evening, they arrive home from work. At night, they go out. In an environment like that, businesses will thrive, since there are people who have immediate access to them. Restaurants will respond to local palates or alternatively will develop them. People will feel safer, since there will be eyes on the street at all hours. Moreover, they will get to know people from walks of life other than their own. Instead of a deteriorating cycle of neighborhood abandonment and rising crime, there will be a cycle of cross-fertilization and mutual protection.

How this cross-fertilization and mutual protection will occur is not predictable. It cannot be planned in advance. Will it be my butcher that warns me that my kids are hanging around with some of the wrong people, or will it be the dry cleaner? Will the restaurant owners press the city for better streetlights, or will the residents? What will the coalition that resists the development of a Wal-Mart superstore look like: will the local bookstore, threatened with being undersold, be in league with residents who want to resist the anonymity of a large chain, or will there be a spontaneous organization of people who meet while cleaning up the streets on Earth Day? The folding, unfolding, and refolding of street life cannot be predicted. It cannot be managed by fiat. One can only help foster a diversity of elements and watch what happens from there. Cities are not matters of function; they are matters of connection. They are rhizomes, not trees. Only this is certain: it is the relationships among the diversity of aspects of urban life that create a vibrant street life, not their segregation into areas of uniformity. Diversity nourishes cities; uniformity strangles them.

And, as in the case of the first Palestinian intifada, the elements that create urban vitality are not themselves identities. Although there is an order, there is no organic whole that is supported by particular elements arranged in a particular way. There are instead local connections that are formed in a variety of ways that change the elements that are connecting.

Objects in cities – whether they are buildings, streets, parks, districts, land-marks, or anything else – can have radically different effects, depending on the circumstances and contexts in which they exist. . . . City dwellings – either existing or potential – are *specific* and particularized buildings *always involved in differing specific processes* such as unslumming, slumming, generation of diversity, self-destruction of diversity.[6]

What is created brings out aspects of people and of the neighborhood that could not have been foreseen, and that were not there in advance. The dynamic interaction that characterizes street life is not a symphony of particular instruments but a chemical process where the elements themselves change their composition as they come into contact with other elements.

Cities are not organic and they are not mechanistic. They are ma-chinic. It is not that no order emerges. An order, an actualization, does emerge. But its emergence has nothing to do with self-subsistent ele-ments arranged according to a pre-given pattern or from connections that are melded once and for all. It emerges from specific contexts of diversity in ways that both create and are created by the elements of that diversity.

[6] Jacobs, *The Death and Life of Great American Cities*, p. 440.

I decide to take up the trumpet because the woman who works at the local record store and with whom I have been passingly flirting played some Clifford Brown on the store sound system the last several times I walked in. I do not begin to play because there was a trumpet player in me waiting for release. It is because our connection created something that was not there before: a desire to take up a musical instrument. Whether I will continue to play depends in good part on what connections I form as I begin. (It may also depend on my talent for playing; but it may not.) Are there teachers who will deepen my interest? Are there local folks who might be interested in playing together? Will there be others around me that reinforce my progress – will, for instance, the woman smile at me a little more often or a little more slyly when she hears that I've started playing?

A successful city allows unity to arise from diversity, not from uniformity. A city that works is an exploration of the virtual. Good city planning fosters that exploration; it does not inhibit it. It is possible, of course, to plan a city in terms of stable identities. It is possible to create a city that mirrors the terms of the dogmatic image of thought. We know what people need, we know how to arrange residences and businesses and places of entertainment in order to meet those needs, and we know how to get them from one place to another most efficiently. Those are the starting points of the dogmatic image of thought as it applies to urban planning. Those are the terms in which thinkers of urban renewal discussed cities, as cities conceived as suburbs, only more crowded and therefore more difficult. The question is whether we can begin to think of cities not in terms of needs we already know but in terms of diversities whose connections we do not yet know.

We must consider cities as actualizations of a virtual difference, as machinic connections, not as the interaction of particular identities, as organic or mechanistic wholes. That is the lesson, although not the vocabulary, of Jane Jacobs' work. It is a lesson we have still not learned. Although the idea of "multi-use" urban geographies is beginning to get a hearing (as though the idea were not over forty years old), we still think of cities in terms of residential, business, and entertainment areas. We still allow our downtowns to become blighted, our neighborhoods to become ghettoized, and our lives to become isolated from those around us. We insulate ourselves rather than forming connections. One can only wonder, given the proliferation of further isolating technologies (television, the internet), whether street life will further decline, or whether, alternatively, the impoverishment that this loss of connection has created will lead to a renewed desire for an urbanism that is Deleuzian rather than dogmatic in its inspiration. Will the future bring us cities or merely less successful suburban enclaves?

IV

Love has its own erotics. It is an erotics that occurs not by representation, and not by communication, but by experimentation and connection. And it occurs not only between individuals but also between parts of individuals, between aspects or surfaces of their bodies.

We often talk of love as though it were a matter solely of individuals and communication. Love happens between two people. It happens when they understand each other, when they arrive at some deeper form of communication. Love is the bonding of two souls that comprehend each other.

This talk is not entirely wrong, just as talk of individual needs in political discussion is not entirely wrong. But it misses large swaths of the event of love. And among the things it misses is love's erotics.

If we think of love solely in terms of communication or understanding, we cannot explain why long-distance relationships are so difficult to maintain. With the advent of the telephone, now supplemented by the internet, communication with one who is far away is simplified. There can always be communication, and perhaps understanding, without the sight, the smell, the sound of the beloved. Why, then, do people need to experience the bodily presence of those they love?

One might say that what is missing is sexuality. True. But what do we mean by sexuality here? Is it simply the act of penetration or the consequence of orgasm? Why is it that when we masturbate we do not experience the same level of joy as when we make love with someone, particularly with someone we care about? Sexuality is itself embedded in a larger realm, a realm we might call *erotics*. When we enter that larger realm, we are no longer in the arena of communication – or better, we are no longer simply in that arena. Nor are we simply at the level of individuals. Instead we are at the level of sub-individual bodily parts.

A hand caresses the flat of a stomach. An eye gazes over strands of hair lying on a pillow. A thigh meets the soft flesh of a buttock. An ear hears a sigh of contentment or relief or pleasure. These are not matters of communication; they are matters of erotics. The hand that caresses the stomach is not telling anything to the stomach, nor to the individual whose stomach it is. It is connecting to the stomach, exploring it. And in doing so it is creating sensations that are not, strictly speaking, either mine or yours or ours. There is no possession of the sensation, and there is no subject of it. If we want to put it in terms of individuals, we might say that each of us is the object of the sensation rather than its subject. But each of us is not the only object. The hand, the stomach: they are also the objects of sensation.

And who is the subject of the caress? Is it the individual, the person who caresses? Not necessarily. If I *decide* to move my hand thus on your stomach, then I, the individual, am the subject of the caress. But must a caress be like this? Must caressing be a conscious endeavor embarked upon by a consciousness? Often, and particularly when love deepens, it does not. I do not caress your stomach. My hand caresses it. Automatically, and without decision. *There is always something outside our identification as subjects and persons.* There is an unconscious erotics of bodies that relies neither on the decisions of particular individuals nor on the mutual projects they have embarked upon. There is not simply a me and a you. Nor is there an us that is the melding of each. There is a hand and a stomach and a sensation arising from their connection.

We can see evidence for this in the heat of sexual passion. We say that people *lose* themselves. That is a good way to put it. In the erotics of the sexual moment, there are no longer two individuals. And this is not because there is a single individual that is the fusion of the two. There are not fewer beings there, but more. There are arms and genitals and ears and eyes and soles and hair and fingertips; there is a series of explorations and connections and experimentations that arise not as decisions but on both the near and far sides of decisions and the individuals who make them. They arise when individuals lose themselves.

It is not only in sexual erotics that there are "many subjects." To hear the sigh of the beloved, say when she is taking a shower, is not simply for one person to hear the pleasure of another. It is for an ear to become the object of a sound, for it to be aroused by noise. If this is communication, then what information is being communicated? What is the content? If this is solely about individuals, then where am I in all this? Am I the vehicle for the sensation, or only its effect? Might it be more accurate to say that at that moment I *arise* out of my aural excitement than that I *experience* it?

Love's erotics is a matter between individuals, but it is not only that. It is also a matter between body parts, between surfaces that come in contact. And the individuals to whom those surfaces belong are a product of that contact at least as much as its subject. Our bodies are the actualization of a virtual that love's erotics explores. Erotics explores the virtual on many levels: the individual, the pre-individual, the between-individuals, the between-individual-parts.

We are taught what is to be thought of as erotic, what we should be aroused by. We all know the images: slim, flowing bodies for women, hard muscular bodies for men. Big breasts, big pecs. Long legs, large quads. But it often does not happen like that. It is often that something else becomes erotic. The eye is caught by the glint of light from a knee. The roughness of a patch of skin becomes provocative to a finger. The bones of an anorexic or the flesh of obesity are compelling. A lisp or a stutter arouses. One part of a body calls out to another, not with information but with invitation. Or better, a relationship of eroticism occurs between them that creates both subjects and objects. There is an event, an event of erotics that arises across and between the surfaces of bodies. It may be a surprise to us to discover these sensations, these arousals. But that is because we still do not know of what a body is capable.

V

Individual lives. Lives of political movements. Lives of cities. Erotic lives. Other lives as well: those of chemicals, of cells, of time, of environments, of languages. And yet still more lives of which we have not spoken. No one has done a Deleuzian analysis of the life of a weather system, although it could be done. All of these lives are actualizations of the virtual, creations of specific identities from swarms of difference.

We have seen here, in the lives of Coltrane, of the first Palestinian intifada, of cities, and of love's erotics, illustrations of living that can be given a Deleuzian reading. They can be given other readings as

well, more traditional ones. But those other readings neglect aspects
of what they are accounting for that Deleuze's approach captures.
Often they miss the most important thing: the unconscious character
of Coltrane's solos or the pre-individual level of erotic sensation.

But it is not simply a matter of accounting for what is there, for what
there is. The question of how one might live is two-fold. It is both a
question of how living might go and of how one might go about living.
The lives we have glanced at in this chapter address the first question,
but not the second. We have seen that living might be a matter of the
actualization of difference. But we know as well that actualizations do
not have to be compelling or significant. They might not yield the Interesting, the Remarkable, or the Important. Most often they do not.
Most saxophonists seek to repeat the identities that have been handed
down to them. The second Palestinian intifada is a violent and often
uncreative affair, even if the occupation it is struggling against is abom-
inable. Cities are often segregated, blighted; sexuality is often rote.

We should not conclude from this, Deleuze argues, that ontology
should give primacy to identity. It is not that identities come first,
difference later. Rather it is that difference is often neglected, the
virtual unexplored. The conformity of our lives has less to do with the
necessity of rigid identities than with the refusal to think, to act, to live
in accordance with a difference that is always there, always subsisting
within the world that is presented to us.

What makes the illustrations we have seen here significant is that
each involves an experimentation that is willing to recognize that it
does not already know what it will find. Each heads resolutely into the
virtual with no guarantee of success. Many people call Coltrane's later
work noise. The jury is still out on the importance of the first intifada.
The diversity of cities can lead to antagonism as well as vibrancy. Erotics
can become obsessive, centripetal, self-destructive. Deleuze cites examples of the dangers of exploration: "Kleist and his suicide pact, Hold-
erlin and his madness, Fitzgerald and his destruction, Virginia Woolf
and her disappearance."[7] To experiment is not necessarily to succeed.
But it is also not to walk away from what is there. A line of flight is
not a flight from reality but a flight within it. It does not create from
nothing but rather experiments with a difference that is immanent to

7 Deleuze and Parnet, *Dialogues*, p. 140.

our world. There is always something more, more than we can know, more than we can perceive. The question before us, and it is a question of living, is whether we are willing to explore it, or instead are content to rest upon its surface.

Deleuze's ontology has not answered the question of how one is to go about living, at least not directly. There are no instructions; there is no handbook. *This is how it should be done: Lodge yourself on a stratum . . .* What he has done instead is to conceive the world in a way that makes conformity not the monolith that needs to be broken but instead the detritus of our possibilities. It is not, on Deleuze's view, deviance that needs to explain itself. Rather it is conformity that should make us raise an eyebrow. Difference is there, always. It is immanent to our present and returning to us from our future. We explore and experiment, not in order to reject this world, but in order better to embrace it.

And so we return to ontology. Foucault and Derrida reject ontology in part because of the conformism it promotes. They are right to reject conformism, but they do not need to reject ontology. If difference is deeper than identity, if actualization proceeds from the virtual, if multiplicity is immanent to our world, then the only ontology that needs to be rejected is an ontology of identity. Ontology has been thought to be an ontology of identity since Plato. But it does not need to be that way. Ontology can be an ontology of difference. It can be an ontology where what is there is not the same old things but a process of continual creation, an ontology that does not seek to reduce being to the knowable but instead seeks to widen thought to palpate the unknowable. An ontology of difference is attuned to the concerns of Derrida and Foucault. It accomplishes the same tasks, using the opposite means. Rather than jettisoning ontology, Deleuze gives it a new meaning.

What might this have to do with the question of how one might live, of how one might go about living? If we seek a prescription, then the answer is: nothing. Deleuze does not answer the ancient question of how one should live. He abandons the modern question of how one should act. He is interested in prescribing neither for our lives nor for our behavior. And yet he *is* interested in normative questions. He is interested in how we act and how our lives go.

The question of how living might go is both an invitation and a provocation. Deleuze's ontology is not for the faint of heart. To experiment in Deleuze's sense, to take his ontology seriously, is not to fill the gaps in our knowledge, nor to seek what we might do on the basis of what we can do. To experiment is to expose those lines of flight that are both of us and not of our identity. It is to explore the virtual without knowing what it will yield. It is to palpate difference in one's thought and in one's living. It is to throw the dice joyously without calculating the numbers that will fall back. To experiment is to ask with the fibers of one's being – the individual fibers, the interpersonal fibers, the pre-individual and supra-individual fibers – the only question Deleuze deems worthy of a life: how might a life go, how might one live?

What Deleuze understands is that the question of how one might live is not like the questions of ancient and modern philosophy. It cannot be answered by means of rules or prescriptions or models or ideals. If one attempts to answer the question of how one might live that way, then one falls back into one of the two earlier questions, either the ancient question or the modern one. What is required is not instruction but invitation, not a directive but an opening. To put it in terms Deleuze would recognize, what we require are not solutions but problems. What Deleuze has put before us is an ontology of problems, an ontology that faces us neither as an explanation of the world nor as a solution to a philosophical question.

Deleuze's ontology is not a resting place; it is not a zone of comfort; it is not an answer that allows us to abandon our seeking. It is the opposite. An ontology of difference is a challenge. To recognize that there is more than we have been taught, that what is presented to us is only the beginning of what there is, puts before us the greater task of our living. We have not finished with living; we are never finished with living. However we live, there is always more. We do not know of what a body is capable, nor how it can live. The alternatives of contentment (*I have arrived*) and hopelessness (*There is nowhere to go*) are two sides of the same misguided thought: that what is presented to us is what there is.

There is more, always more.

Further Reading

In what follows, I point some directions for readers interested in reading more about Deleuze, his interlocutors, or the issues that have arisen in the course of this book. I include bibliographical details for texts that have not been cited in the previous pages. As far as general treatments of Deleuze's thought, Claire Colebrook's *Gilles Deleuze* and John Rajchman's *The Deleuze Connections* are excellent books. The former is more literary and cinematic in its orientation; the latter is more difficult, and perhaps better approached after some engagement with Deleuze's writings.

Chapter 1

Regarding the questions of *How should one live?* and *How should one act?* Plato and Aristotle are obvious cases of the former, while Kant is exemplary of the latter. Plato's *Republic* and Aristotle's *Nichomachean Ethics* offer overviews of how each thinker approaches the question of how one should live. There are a number of extant translations of these works. Kant's *Critique of Practical Reason* (tr. Lewis White Beck, Indianapolis: Bobbs-Merrill, 1956) or his shorter *Groundwork of the Metaphysic of Morals* (tr. H. J. Paton, New York: Harper & Row, 1956) offer as rigorous approaches to the second question as one is likely to find. Regarding Nietzsche, the two texts most influential on Deleuze's thought are probably *Thus Spoke Zarathustra* (included in *The Portable Nietzsche*, ed. and tr. Walter Kaufman, New York: Viking Press, 1954) and *On the Genealogy of Morals*. Sartre's humanism receives its summary statement in his essay "Existentialism" in *Existentialism and Human Emotions* (New York: Philosophical Library, 1957); his technical treatment appears in *Being and Nothingness: A Phenomenological Essay on Ontology* (tr. Hazel Barnes, New York: Philosophical Library, 1956). Foucault's primary genealogical works, in which the rejection of ontology appears most forthrightly, are *Discipline and Punish* and the first volume of *The History of Sexuality* (tr. Robert Hurley, New York: Vintage Books, 1980). Derrida has had a long and prolific writing career; my own preference is for his early works, for instance *Speech and Phenomena and Other Essays on Husserl's Theory of Signs* (tr. David Allison, Evanston: Northwestern University Press, 1973) and *Writing and Difference* (tr. Alan Bass, Chicago: University of Chicago Press, 1978).

Chapter 2

Spinoza's central work is the *Ethics*, of which there are several translations. Bergson's *Matter and Memory* (tr. N. M. Paul and W. S. Palmer, New York: Zone Books, 1988) is often appealed to by Deleuze, and forms the basis for the treatment discussed here. The most important existential/phenomenological discussion of time is Husserl's *The Phenomenology of Internal Time-Consciousness* (ed. Martin Heidegger, tr. James S. Churchill, Bloomington: Indiana University Press, 1964). Nietzsche's books have already been cited. Among Deleuze's works, *Expressionism in Philosophy: Spinoza, Spinoza: Practical Philosophy, Bergsonism*, and *Nietzsche and Philosophy* are the key treatments of Spinoza, Bergson, and Nietzsche respectively.

Chapter 3

Unfortunately, very little of Gilbert Simondon's work has been translated into English. However, the introduction to *L'individu et sa genèse physico-biologique* appears in Crary and Kwinter's *Incorporations*. Monod's *Chance and Necessity* and Prigogine and Stengers' *Order Out of Chaos* are difficult texts, but important for understanding Deleuze's approach to science. Regarding language, Saussure's *Course in General Linguistics* is probably the single most influential linguistics text of the twentieth century, at least as far as Europe is concerned. Lewis Carroll's *Alice in Wonderland* and *Through the Looking Glass* provide Deleuze with numerous examples of nonsense; Martin Gardner's *The Annotated Alice* is an excellent guide through those texts. Deleuze's approach to science appears in various places in *Difference and Repetition* (many of them cited in the above pages) as well as in his later collaboration with Guattari, *A Thousand Plateaus*, especially Plateau 3. The dogmatic image of thought is the subject of the third chapter of *Difference and Repetition*. The key text for Deleuze's early approach to language is *The Logic of Sense*. Later, in his collaboration with Guattari, he develops an approach that is different from, but not at odds with, the earlier one discussed in the present book. The fourth of the thousand plateaus discusses the later approach at length.

Chapter 4

There are a number of statements of liberalism, but perhaps two stand out above others: John Stuart Mill's nineteenth-century work *On Liberty* (Indianapolis: Hackett, 1978) and John Rawls's *A Theory of Justice* (Cambridge: Harvard University Press, 1971). Among communitarian works, Michael Sandel's *Liberalism and the Limits of Justice* is an excellent example. Marx and Marxism, of course, have a long and complex history. As far as Marx's writings, the earlier *Economic and Philosophic Manuscripts* (which can be found, among other places, in *Early Writings*, tr. Rodney Livingstone and Gregor Benton, New York: Random House, 1975) and the later *Capital: Volume One* (tr. Ben Fowkes, New York: Random House, 1977) are representative works. Foucault's *Discipline and Punish* has already been cited. Much of Deleuze's overtly political writings are done in collaboration with Félix Guattari: *Anti-Oedipus* (especially the fourth chapter) and *A Thousand Plateaus* (especially Plateaus 9, 12, and 13), as well as *Kafka: Toward a Minor Literature*, which has a discussion in the third chapter of minority and becoming-minor in literature. My discussion has also relied on the fourth chapter of Deleuze's *Dialogues* with Claire Parnet.

Chapter 5

There have been many things written about John Coltrane, but for an overview of his music and his style, I prefer the video *The World According to John Coltrane* (New York: BMG Video, 1991). Among its virtues is a grainy video of a performance of "My Favorite Things" that captures Coltrane's searching music as well as anything I have seen. Jane Jacobs' *The Death and Life of Great American Cities* remains the touchstone for thinking about the character of cities. The Palestinian intifada has also been the subject of much study. One book that offers an early overview of the first intifada is Don Peretz's *Intifada* (Boulder: Westview, 1991). For more recent developments, I have co-edited a book with Muna Hamzeh, *Operation Defensive Shield: Witnesses to Israeli War Crimes* (London: Pluto Press, 2003), that focuses on Israel's 2002 invasion of the territories, but also offers a more general treatment of the issues. Regarding erotics, the early pages of *Anti-Oedipus* have an excellent discussion of couplings that are not person to person, but part to part.

References

Bergson, Henri. *Matter and Memory*, tr. N. M. Paul and W. S. Palmer. New York: Zone Books, 1988 (first published 1908).

Boundas, Constantin. "Deleuze-Bergson: An Ontology of the Virtual," from *Deleuze: A Critical Reader*, ed. Paul Patton. Oxford: Basil Blackwell, 1996.

Carroll, Lewis. *The Annotated Alice*, with notes by Martin Gardner. New York: World Publishing, 1960.

Colebrook, Claire. *Gilles Deleuze*. New York: Routledge, 2002.

Commoner, Barry. "Unraveling the DNA Myth," *Harper's*, February 2002, pp. 39–47.

Deleuze, Gilles. *Bergsonism*, tr. Hugh Tomlinson and Barbara Habberjam. New York: Zone Books, 1988 (first published 1966).

———. "La conception de la différence chez Bergson," *Les études bergsoniennes*, vol. 4, 1956, p. 88.

———. *Difference and Repetition*, tr. Paul Patton. New York: Columbia University Press, 1994 (first published 1968).

———. *Empiricism and Subjectivity*, tr. Constantin Boundas. New York: Columbia University Press, 1991.

———. *Expressionism in Philosophy: Spinoza*, tr. Martin Joughin. New York: Zone Press, 1990 (first published 1968).

———. *Foucault*, tr. Sean Hand. Minneapolis: University of Minnesota Press, 1988 (first published 1986).

———. "Immanence: A Life," in *Pure Immanence: Essays on a Life*, tr. Anne Boyman. New York: Zone Press, 2001 (essay first published 1995), pp. 25–33.

———. *Kant's Critical Philosophy: The Doctrine of the Faculties*, tr. Hugh Tomlinson. Minneapolis: University of Minnesota Press, 1985 (first published 1963).

———. *The Logic of Sense*, tr. Mark Lester and Charles Stivale. New York: Columbia University Press, 1990 (first published 1969).

————. *Nietzsche and Philosophy*, tr. Hugh Tomlinson. New York: Columbia University Press, 1983 (first published 1962).

————. "Nomad Thought," tr. David Allison. From *The New Nietzsche: Contemporary Styles of Interpretation*. New York: Dell, 1977 (essay first published 1973), pp. 142–9.

————. "Postscript on Societies of Control," in *Negotiations 1972–1990*, tr. Martin Joughin. New York: Columbia University Press, 1995.

————. *Proust and Signs*, tr. Richard Howard. New York: George Braziller, 1972.

Deleuze, Gilles, and Guattari, Felix. *Anti-Oedipus: Capitalism and Schizophrenia*, tr. Robert Hurley, Mark Seem, and Helen R. Lane. New York: Viking Press, 1977 (first published 1972).

————. *Kafka: Toward a Minor Literature*, tr. Dana Polan. Minneapolis: University of Minnesota Press, 1986 (first published 1975).

————. *A Thousand Plateaus*, tr. Brian Massumi. Minneapolis: University of Minnesota Press, 1987 (first published 1980).

————. *What Is Philosophy?* tr. Hugh Tomlinson and Graham Burchell. New York: Columbia University Press, 1994 (first published 1991).

Deleuze, Gilles, and Parnet, Claire. *Dialogues*, tr. Hugh Tomlinson and Barbara Habberjam. New York: Columbia University Press, 1987 (first published 1977).

Descartes, René. *Passions of the Soul*, tr. Stephen Voss. Indianapolis: Hackett, 1990.

Foucault, Michel. *Discipline and Punish*, tr. Alan Sheridan. New York: Random House, 1977 (first published 1975).

————. "Practicing Criticism," an interview with Didier Eribon, tr. Alan Sheridan. From *Michel Foucault: Politics, Philosophy, Culture*, ed. Lawrence Kritzman. New York: Routledge, 1988, pp. 152–6.

————. "Truth, Power, Self: An Interview with Michel Foucault," from *Technologies of the Self: A Seminar with Michel Foucault*. Amherst: University of Massachusetts Press, 1988, pp. 9–15.

Husserl, Edmund. *The Phenomenology of Internal Time-Consciousness*, ed. Martin Heidegger, tr. James S. Churchill. Bloomington: Indiana University Press, 1964.

Jacobs, Jane. *The Death and Life of Great American Cities*. New York: Vintage, 1961.

May, Todd. "Deleuze, Difference, and Science." From *Continental Philosophy and Science*, ed. Gary Gutting. Oxford: Basil Blackwell, 2004.

Monod, Jacques. *Chance and Necessity: An Essay on the Natural Philosophy of Modern Biology*, tr. Austryn Wainhouse. New York: Knopf, 1971 (first published 1970).

Nietzsche, Friederich. *On the Genealogy of Morals*, tr. Douglas Smith. Oxford: Oxford University Press, 1996 (first published 1887).

————. *Thus Spoke Zarathustra*. (First published 1892.) From *The Portable Nietzsche*, tr. and ed. Walter Kaufmann. New York: Viking Press, 1954.

————. *The Will to Power*, ed. Walter Kaufmann, tr. Walter Kaufmann and R. J. Hollingdale. New York: Random House, 1967.

Pearson, Keith Ansell. *Germinal Life: The Difference and Repetition of Deleuze*. New York: Routledge, 1999.

Prigogine, Ilya, and Stengers, Isabelle. *La Nouvelle Alliance: Métamorphose de la science*. Paris: Gallimard, 1979.

———. *Order Out of Chaos: Man's New Dialogue With Nature*. Boulder and London: New Science Library, 1984.

Proust, Marcel. *Remembrance of Things Past: The Past Recaptured*, tr. Andreas Mayor. New York: Random House, 1970 (first published 1927).

Rajchman, John. *The Deleuze Connections*. Cambridge: MIT Press, 2000.

Sandel, Michael. *Liberalism and the Limits of Justice*. Cambridge: Cambridge University Press, 1982.

Sartre, Jean-Paul. "Existentialism," tr. Bernard Frechtman. From *Existentialism and Human Emotions*. New York: Philosophical Library, 1957, pp. 9–51.

Saussure, Ferdinand de. *Course in General Linguistics*, ed. Charles Bally and Albert Sechehaye, tr. Wade Baskin. New York: McGraw-Hill, 1959.

Simondon, Gilbert. "The Genesis of the Individual," tr. Mark Cohen and Sanford Kwinter. From *Zone 6: Incorporations*, ed. S. Kwinter and J. McCrary. New York: Zone Books, 1992, pp. 297–319.

Spinoza, Benedictus de. *The Ethics and Selected Letters*, ed. Seymour Feldman, tr. Samuel Shirley. Indianapolis: Hackett, 1982 (first published 1677).

Williams, Bernard. *Ethics and the Limits of Philosophy*. Cambridge: Harvard University Press, 1985.

Wittgenstein, Ludwig. *Philosophical Investigations*, tr. G. E. M. Anscombe. New York: Macmillan, 1953.

Index

2772706R00099

Printed in Great Britain
by Amazon.co.uk, Ltd.,
Marston Gate.